NUMBER 460

THE ENGLISH EXPERIENCE

ITS RECORD IN EARLY PRINTED BOOKS PUBLISHED IN FACSIMILE

The publishers acknowledge their gratitude to
the Curators of the Bodleian Library, Oxford
for their permission to reproduce
the Library's copy, Shelfmark: Douce G.32

Library of Congress Catalog Card Number:
70-38197

S.T.C.No. 12020
Collation: a-p^8

Published in 1972 by

Theatrvm Orbis Terrarvm Ltd.,
O.Z.Voorburgwal 85, Amsterdam

&

Da Capo Press Inc.
-a subsidiary of Plenum Publishing Corporation-
277 West 17th Street, New York N.Y. 10011

Printed in the Netherlands
ISBN 90 221 0460 5

HOW
SVPERIOR
POWERS OGHT TO
BE OBEYD OF THEIR
subiects: and wherin they may lawfully by Gods worde be disobeyed
and resisted.

Wherin also is declared the cause of all this pre
sent miserie in England, and the onely way
to remedy the same.

BY CHRISTOPHER GOODMAN.

¶ The Lord hath broght vpon them à nation from a
farre contrey, an impudent nation and of a strange
langage. Baruch 4. Deut.28.

Printed at Geneua by Iohn Crispin.

M. D. LVIII.

VVILLIAM VVHITIN-

GHAM TO ALL THEM

that loue to knoVVe the trueth
and foloVVe it: Grace and peace.

Gnorance the mother of
error and profeſſed enne-
mie to Gods Trueth, hath
two daughters by whoſe
flatteries and ſubtile practi
ſes ſhe blyndeth mens eyes,
obſcureth the Trueth, and
withdraweth vs from the way of knollage:
Cuſtome, and Negligence. Wherof the firſt
ſo bewitcheth vs, that althogh we wallowe
and walter in darcke blyndenes, yet as it
were by dreaming we ſeme to walke in the
bright ſunne ſhyning : ſo that Cuſtome and
compagnie may farre ſoner drawe vs to per
dition , then Trueth and reaſon bring vs to
the vnderſtanding of our error . The other
being a domeſtical ſeruante and wel ac-
quaynted with our maners, by crafty flatte-
rie doth ouercome vs . For the fleſhe is prowde and ſwelleth againſt God , ſhe glorieth
in her owne wiſdome, ſhe loueth her owne
conſel, ſhe deliteth in her owne imaginatiõ
and poſicie : and albeit we knowe that
ſlothful Negligence is an impediment and
blocke in our nature to ſtoppe vs from
Trueth: yet willingly we gyue place to her

a. ii.

4

flattering perſuaſions, and ſuffre her to trayne vs to wilful deſtruction. So that betwixt
Cuſtome and Negligence we rather holde
with damnable Ignorance, and wiſſhe to be
plonged in abominable errors, then by diligent ſtudy and ſerching of the Trueth learne to knoꝛe our duetie to God, ād what he
requireth of vs to do towardes our neighbour. Then if we wolde auoyde theſe euils,
we muſt loue and embrace the cōtrary ver-
tues : and if Cuſtome be wicked and withholde vs from God, we muſt ſpedely reiect
her and cleaue vnto God: and if Negligence
haue noſeled vs in the denne of Ignorance,
we muſt purchaſe by diligence to proffit in
the ſchole of knollage . For the acheuing
wherof (whē M. Chriſtopher Goodman one
of our miniſters , according to the courſe of
the text , expounded bothe faithfully and
cōfortably this place of the Actes of the A-
poſtles, *Iudge whether it b iuſte before God*
to obey you rather then God) certeyne lear -
ned and godly men moſte inſtantly , and at
ſondry tymes required hī to dilate more at
large that his Sermon , and to ſuffre it to be
printed, that not onely we here preſent, but
our bretherne in England and other places
might be perſuaded in the trueth of that doc
trine concerninge obedience to the magiſ-
trat, and ſo glorifie God with vs. Whiche re-
queſt he admitted not eaſely, til at lēgth wel
wayinge how many periſhed in their ignorance

Act. 4. d.

rance for lack of meanes to attaine to the
knollage of the trueth: and also conferringe
his articles and chief propositions with the
best learned in these partes (who approued
them) he cōsented to enlarge the said Sermō
and so to print it, as a token of his duetie
and good affection towarde the Churche of
God: and then if it were thoght good to
the iudgement of the godly, to translate the
same into other lāgages that the profit ther
of might be more vniuersal. Ther is no doute but many ouercome with olde Custome,
or yelding to negligēt Slothfulnes wil ether
dispraise this profitable worke, or neglect
it. For euel Custome deliting in Ignorance
wil straight way flie to her wonted argumēt: What is this newe doctrine? and whē-
ce is it? Negligence on the other part crieth
maliciously: We haue bookes ynough:
what nede we yet to be set to schole? Thus
Satan with double subteltie deludeth the
worlde, keping his euer so fast tyed in the
bandes of blynde Ignorance, that they can
nether stirre hand nor fote: they are blynde
and can not se what is good: and thogh it
be offered, yet are they insensible and can
not fele it. The trueth of Gods worde is to
them moste odious: but mans dreames and
deuils doctrines are in greate estimatiō and
reuerence. Their false prophets and papistical priests haue so charmed them, that I-
gnorance is holden for knollage, error for

Mat. 1 c.
Act. 17. e

a. iii.

trueth , superstition for religion, disobedience for obedience, the Masse for the Lordes Supper , Purgatorie for Chrits blood, **2.Cor.11.d** workes for faith , Belial for God , and as S. Paul saieth , If they bring you into slauerie, ye endure it: if they deuoure you, ye suffre it: if they spoile you of your goods , ye are content : if they preferre them selues and thrust you downe, ye forbeare it: if they smite you on the face , yet ye can susteine it . And thus the children of Satan had rather rot in their barbarous ignorance , then by submitting thē selues to the mercies of God, aspire to the perfect vnderstanding of his heauenly will reueiled vnto vs by his worde. But thou the sonne of God , shewe thy duetie and loue towarde thy merciful Father , endeuour to knowe his wil, declare thy affection towardes his Scriptures , be zealous of his glorie, reuerence his ministers, and receaue thankfully his graces geuen to his Churche by them . Proue diligently and trie by the tou- **2.Cor.2. d.** chstone who speake the wordes of God in pure simplicitie as in Gods presēce, and who choppe and change the same, making marchandise therof to traffique according to mans pleasure . Nether do we desire onely that you shulde be persuaded in this trueth because we our selues so beleue : but we ex- **Ioh. 4. f.** hort you, that as the Samaritās dyd not onely beleue in our Sauiour Christ because of the womās report which broght the newes,

but

but forafmuche as they them felues heard
him, and knewe that Chrift was the Sauiour
of the worlde: fo whē you fhal wel examine
thefe things by the rule of Gods worde, you
wolde not fo much by our report as by your
owne iudgement and knowlage credit the
trueth. Remēbring that the worthy people
of Beroe were cōmēded by the holy Goft, be *Act. 17. e.*
caufe they tryed by Gods worde whether
the minifters preachīg agreed with the fame
or no. Seing then by thefe examples we are
bonde to feke the wil of God manifefted
vnto vs in his Scriptures, what excufe fhal
we alledge for our pretenfed ignorance? Beholde here thou heareft the Eternal fpeaking by his minifter, in whofe mouthe he
hath put his worde, and whofe lippes muft
kepe the Lawe ād the vnderftāding therof, as
wryteth the Prophet Malachie. Beware ther *Chap. 2. a*
fore that thou neglect not him that brīgeth
the worde of God, but quickely gyue eare ād
obey. For if thou defireft to knowe thy due
tie to thy Prince, and his charge likewife
ouer thee, read this book and thou fhalt wel
vnderftāde both: If thou wifhe for Chriftiā
libertie, come and fe how it may eafely be
had: If thou woldeft loue God aboue man,
here thou fhalt knowe how to obey God ra
ther then mā. Let the Apoftles of Chrift here
be thy fchole maifters, and then the more
thou learneft: the leffe occafiō fhalt thou haue to repent. Obedience is neceffarie where

God is glorified , but if God be diſhonored thy obedience is abominable in the ſight of God, be it neuer ſo beautiful in mans eyes. Gods worde is our guyde to leade vs in our doings : when it commandeth vs to obey God, we muſt diſobey man in the contrary: for no man can ſerue two maiſters : and when our heauély maiſter cõmandeth obedience to man , it is euer to be vnderſtand, in the Lord. So that obedience to Gods Lawes by diſſobeyíg más wicked lawes is mu che commendable , but to diſobey God for any duetie to mã is all to gether damnable: as in the diſcourſe of this booke thou ſhalt fully be aſſeured , if God open thyn eyes to ſe the trueth, ãd moue thy heart to embrace it . The Spirit of God, which is the ſcholemaiſtre to leade vs into all trueth , lighten your hartes, gyue you myndes to vnderſtande , and courage to execute his holy wil , to the ſetting forth of Chriſtes kingdome , the proffit of his Churche and confuſion of Satans power and Antichriſts . Amen . From Geneua this firſt of Ianuarie. 1558.

THE

AS there is nothige to be cópared to true obediéce, in preseruíge the cómó welth of townes, cities, and kingdoms: or in maynteyninge true religió, Christiã peace & cócorde (for therby euery mã is instructed how to render vnto God his due honour & glorie: & to man that, whiche his office requireth) Eué so is ther nothinge more hatefull to God, nether more hurtefull to mã, then so to be bewitched with Satans false illusions, that they are not able to put difference betwyxte obedience & disobedience : but as men without all iudgemét and naturall sense, take thone for thother, beinge in them selues playne contrarie, whiche is the onelie cause of all disorder and lamentable confusion, where with the whole worlde is bothe this daie, and hath bene also fró the beginning, most miserably defaced and oppressed. For when vile man, replenished with pride, vayne glorie, and grosse ignorance, will measure obedience with the crowked lyne of his owne corrupte iudge-

True obedience rendreth to God due honor & also to man as his office requireth. What great daunger it is, not to put differéce betwene obedience and disobedience.

ment, and not with the infallible trueth
of Goddes holie worde, he muſt nedes
preferre his owne decrees, phantaſies,
and ordináces, to the cófortable Lawes
and liuelie preceptes of God his creator.
Then in place of iuſtice, he receaueth
iniuſtice, for right wronge, for vertue
vice, for lawe will, for loue hatred, for
trueth falſhod, for playne dealing diſſi-
mulation, for religion ſuperſtition, for

whatplags
come for di
ſobediéce.

true worſhippe deteſtable idolatrie:
and to be ſhorte, for God Sathan, for
Chriſt Antichriſt, and with him ſuche
plages of God, and diſorder amonge
mé, as are this daye ſet before oure eyes
to beholde in all places throughout the
vniuerſal worlde, and haue bene likewiſe euen from the beginninge. When

Gen.3.

Adam was placed in paradiſe, beinge a
creature moſte perfecte, and abundinge
in all wiſdome and heauenlie knowledge, and wolde at the perſuaſion of his

Adam diſo
beied God
and was
greuouſlie
puniſhed.

wif meaſure obedience rather by his o-
wne reaſon, then by the worde & ſen-
tence of God before pronounced: behold, he was not onelie ſpoyled of wiſdome & knowledge, becomminge a verie foole, in compariſon of that, whiche
                                                    he

he was before : but also sodaynlie destitute of all other singuler giftes, as of
innocencie, and immortalitie, was con-
foūded at the voyce of the Lord, assha-
med at his owne nakednesse , and felt
the dredfull indignation and curse of
God, whiche he had procured, not onelie to him self, but broght the same also
vpon all his posteritie after him . When
the whole worlde was so corrupted in
their owne wayes in the dayes of faithfull Noha, no regarde was at all to the
obedience of the liuinge Lorde, nor yet
to the godlie admonitions of iust Noha:
but euerie man was so drowned in his
owne lustes , that the space of an hundreth & twenty yeares was not sufficiēt
to moue them to repentance . And therfore could they not escape the strange
and horrible iudgement of God, whiche
immediatlie after folowed moste iustlie.
And althogh in that wicked generation
abonded all kinde of wickednesse , as
well agaynst God as man , in so muche
as the earthe then might be compted a
verie hell, yet from whence proceaded
all this rebellion against Goddes mightie maiestie , but onelie for that they

All makin
de was iust
ly punished
for Adams
disobediēce

Gen. 6.

The worl-
de plaged
in Nohas
dayes for
disobediēce

The cause
of all diso-
bedience
is, not to
measure ou
re doings
by Godds
worde.
Rom.2.

measured all thinges after their owne
corrupt reason, and not by his holie Lawes and preceptes? Whiche they had
now receaued of their forefathers, hearde of Noah, yea, and had them ingraf-
ted naturally in their hartes.   The pro-
bation wherof might easilie be deduced
from all ages euen to oure tyme by in-
numerable and euident examples, if it
were nedefull in so playne a matter.

we must
not measu
re our obe-
dience af-
ter our ou-
ne phante-
sies.

For who is so blynde that maye not se
how man sheweth his rebellion, neuer
so muche, as when he woulde be moste
obedient in his owne sight and iudgement? not measuringe the same by
the streght lyne and true touchestone,
whiche is the Lawe and worde of God,
but suffringe him self to be led by his
owne corrupte iudgemét and affectiós.

This turned the Wisdome of the
Gentiles into mere folishnesse, inuétin-
ge shamefull idolatrye for true worshipp, as witnessethe the Apostle.

Rom.1.

Mat.15.

This blynded the Ieues with hy-
pocrisie and cloked holynesse, makinge
the Lawe of the liuinge Lorde to geue
place to their inuented traditions by
man. Out of this stinkinge puddle of

Disobe-
dience

mans

mans brayne haue iſſued forthe ſo great diuerſitie of opinions and daungerous heriſies, wherwith the Churche
of God hathe bé at all tymes horriblye
tormented. Finallie from hence hathe
Antichriſte filled his peſtilente cupp of
all ſortes of deadlie poyſon, where of he
hathe made the whole earthe almoſt,
and her kinges and Princes, not onelie
to drinke : but to be moſt vilelie ouercome and dronken. In whoſe defence
they haue armed them ſelues againſt
the Lorde ãd Chriſte his Son : who notwithſtanding with impudent mouthes
they profeſſe, where as in verie dede
they perſecute him moſte cruellie in his
Sainɔts by all means poſſible, fightinge, as men in a rage, vnder the banner
of that filthie beaſt. And yet theſe men
in the middle of their furie, without all
obedience & ordre, ſubuertinge the Lawes of God and of nature, will be called notwithſtandinge the defenders of
the faithe, mayntayners of true religió,
autours of peace, teachers of obedience, ãd moſt diſcrete gouernours of common weales and policies. To the intent
therfore that theſe diſguiſed perſonnes

is the
puddle of
all heriſies
and error.

Apo. 17.
Antichriſte
is the pla-
ge of God
for mãs diſ
obedience.

Pſal. 2.

The tyrats
are Anti-
chriſtes tor
mentours
and perſe-
cute Chriſt

(whiche abufe the whole worlde) may
appeare in their owne liuely fhape, and
be knowen as they are in dede, I haue
thoght it good, hauing occafion by
this worthie anfwere of Peter and Iohn, and beinge hereto of diuers godlie
perfons prouoked, fomewhat to wryte
of true obedience: to wit, what God
him felf requiereth of vs, and what he
commandethe to be geuen alfo to men.
Wherby (God wi: ge) the difguifed
clokes, and craftie pretences of obedience, vfed and practifed by the vngod
lie worldlings, fhalbe difcouered: who
haue foght alwayes, and yet do feeke
vnder the pleafant name of obedience, onlie to mayntayne their ambition,
pride and libertie: wherby we fhall learne alfo how in tymes paft we haue
bene fhamfullie abufed in yelding to
the willfull wil of man, in obeying his
vngodlie commandements, and fearinge man more then God: and finallie
how it behoueth vs to repent oure former ignoraunce, and with diligence to
redreffe the fame, hauinge more lighte
and fuller knowledge.

Peter and

The occafion wherefore this treatife was writ:, and what profit we may gather therof.

PETER AND IOHN

thē, and said : Whether it be right
in the sight of God to obey you
rather thē God, iudge you. Act. 4.

CHAP. I.

¶ *To whome this answere was geuen, and vpon*
what occasion, how litle the malice of the Iues
preuailed agaynst thiis Apostles, in sekinge to
stopp the Gospell by their crasiie fetches and
chastisynges.

T O the end we may haue
more sensible fealing
of all these things, let
vs diligentlie consider
this answere of S. Peter
& Iohn : aswell to whō
it was made, as vpon what occasion.
After that these ii Apostles, through
the malice of the Priests, the Gouerno-
ure of the Téple and the Sadduces, were violentlie throwne into prison the
night before, for preaching to the
people at Ierusalem in the porche of
Salomon, the resurrection from death
in the Name of Iesus : and the next

The circū
stance of
the answe
re wayed.

Act. 4.

daye folowige were fet forthe, ãd pre-
fented to the whole Senate and Concile of Ierufalem, where was affembled
all the chief Rulers and Elders of the
people of Ifraell, Annas alfo the hie
Prieft, añd Caiaphas, ãd Iohn, and Ale-
xandre, men of great reputation, with
others of the kinred of the high Bif-
fhopp, to be examined of thé, in whofe
name or power they had cured the lame criple (who beinge aboue 40 yeres olde, and lame from his birthe was
daylie broght to the porche of Salo-
mõ to begge his almes) Peter replenif-
fhed with the holie Spirit, ãfwered withe great boldneffe, that they wroght
that miracle in the Name and power
of Iefus Chrift the true Nazarit, Whome the Ieues had crucified, and God
had rayfed from the death: in fo muche as the mouthes of the whole Concile were ftopped & had nothinge to
faye againft them, but as men aftunnif-
fhed wondred at the conftant bol-
deneffe of Peter and Iohn in their anfwere. Then (faithe S. Luke) did the
whole Concile, that is, all thefe fore-
named Magiftrates by common con-
ſent

sent straytelie charge the Apostels
Peter and Iohn , hereafter not so
muche as once to speake to anie man,
muche lesse to preache in the Name of
Iesus: thinking by this means to stoppe
the course of the Gospell, ad hinder the
glorie of Christ, whó they before had
crucified as a malefactor and blasphe-
mer of Gods Name . And althoghe
they were destitute of all reason and
Scripture to answere the Apostles, who
had all redie cófounded thé: yet throu-
ghe auctoritie and ponishméte, whiche
they threatned , they thoght craftelie
to put the Apostles to silence, and so at
length to obtayne the victorie . As we
see this daye the Papistes their succes-
sors, expresse enimies of the Gospel, ád
sworne soldiars of Antichriste , euery
where practise , who beinge ouercome
with the manifest Scriptures , and their
blasphemous mouthes stopped with the
truthe of Gods worde , fight notwithstanding maliciouslie agaynst Christe
withpower, auctoritie, threatnyngs, hor
rible ponishmentes , and cruell murther, resemblinge that old serpét, whose broude they are , whiche was a mur-

The magistrats cómande the Apostles not to preach Christe.

The papists suecead the Iewes in malice ád persecuttó.

Papists are the generation of Vipers. Iohn. 8.

b.

therer from the begyninge.

But when the whole aſſembly had
craftelie côſulted, and wrought all that
they coulde agaynſt the faithfull ſeruã-
tes of God:they were neuer the leſſe diſ
apoynted of their porpoſe . For the glo
rie of Chriſte more brightelie ſhyned,
and the truthe of his Goſpell was better
knowen ãd farther publiſhed, and their
falſhod and raginge madneſſe more eſ-
pied, and abhorred of the godlie . For
what extreame madneſſe was this to ſet
them ſelues agaynſt God, ſo to truſte in
their owne power as thoughe they were
able to reſyſte and ouercome the power
of the all mightie,whiche is the Goſpell
of oure Sauiour Ieſus Chriſte (as wit-
neſſe the the Apoſtle) To thinke that
the threatnings of mê,ſhulde more preuayle with the Apoſtels of Chriſte ,
thenthe threatnings of God ãd his horrible iudgementes apoynted for the di-
ſobediêt?Coulde not the Iewes diſtroye
Chriſte and his doctrine,whiles he was
mortall and liued amongeſt them in
the fleſhe , to whom they did almoſte
what they liſt , an yet would after
thinke

The Goſ-
pell increa
ſeth when
it is perſe-
cuted.

Rom.1.

We muſt
rather fe-
are Goddes
iudgemêts
then mans
threatnyn-
gs.

thinke to bringe it to paſſe, when he
was riſen agayne by his mightie power, and made immortall? Yf they coulde
not keape him in the graue for al their
diligent watche, when he was dead and
buried: thinke they it poſſible to pluke
him downe from heaue̅, from the right-
hande of his father, where he ſitteth and
reigneth in euerlaſtige glorie? Oh vayne and fooliſhe men: he hathe ouercome al readie the whole world, and caſt
forthe of it the Chief Prince & Ruler
Satan, who is no more able to preuay-
le agaynſt his truthe and ſeruauntes. A- *Chriſte a̅d*
re you more ſubtile or ſtronger then Sa *his word*
tan, who is your lorde and maiſter ſo *are inuin-*
longe as you fight agaynſt Chriſte the *ſible.*
Sonne of God? Coulde not ſo mightie a
Prince with ſtande his power, and you
leawde ſouldiars of his, wil thike to op
tayne the victorie? Deathe, whiche no
man can eſcape, coulde not holde
him, neither the power of hell præuay-
le agaynſt him: and yet would you haue him at your commandement, moſte maliciouſlie and traitrouſlie ſigh-
fightinge againſt his ho̅nor, who ſoght

by all means, and yet doth, to do you good and saue you? But ô miserable and vile wretches, double is your condemnation in the fight of God, which not contented to forsake Christe your selues, do so maliciously with your threatenings labour to frustrate others of his moste confortable graces. Full wel doth our Sauiour Christ paynt forth your raginge enuie, sainge, Wo be to you Scribes, Pharisies, and hypocrites, because you shutt the kingdome of heauen before men, not entering your selues, neither wil you suffer such as come, to enter.

Mat. 23.

CHAP. II.

¶ *How the papisticall Churche and Conciles can not but erre, and how they beinge compared to the Iewes, are no lesse deniers and blasphemers of Christ, then the Iewes.*

Great occasions of repentance offered to the Iewes.

I wil not here rehearse what iuste occasió of repentance was offered to this whole assemblie of the Iewes (if their hartes had not bene hardened) as wel by the playne and sensible doctrine

doctrine taught by the Apoftels, whiche they coulde not improue with all their learninge: as by the mightie powere of God declared in fo manie and wonderful miracles wroght by them in the name of Chrifte to côfirme his Gofpel and refurrection, whiches the Iewes notwithftâding ftubbernly did reiecte: Nether yet wil I fpeake of the ftrange defection and notable falling awaie from God amongeft them in Ierufalem, whiche at that tyme (in the iudgement of mâ) appeared to be the onelie Churche of God, to whom appartayned the promifes, who of al other nations had the Lawe, and Prophetes to inftructe them, who onelie profeffed the true and euerliuinge God : and yet amongeft them all that were affembled, was not fo muche as one man to ftande vpon Chriftes parte with the Apoftels, but cô fented and agreed with one accorde, that in the Name of Chrifte they fhulde preache no more to the people. Onelie this I woulde put you in remembrance of, before we proceade anie further, how vayne and vncertayne the doctrine of the blafphemous Papiftes is, whi-

An horrible falling awaye frô God.

Rom 3. and 9.

The Iewefhe churche errethe.

che is grounded vpon no other foundation, then vpon the auctoritie of their
Churche, their Councils, and decrees
of men. And here in dare I make the pa
pistes them selues iudges, whether their
Churche be of more auctoritie or anti-
quite, then was the Churche of the Iewes whiche was the first of all, ād auctorised by God immediatlie: Or whither
their Concils at the appoyntment of
the Romishe Antichriste, were more or-
derlie called and assembled, then was
this Concil holden at Ierusalem by the
appoyntmēt of the Chief priest and Bis
hopp? As for their Churche, the Iewes had the manifeste worde and promesse of God: yea, there was no other
Churche, then visible vpon the earthe,
besides that whiche the Apostels then
began to buylde vpon the true coner-
stone Iesus Christe: where as the papistes haue not so muche as one worde
or promesse to proue that they are (as
they impudentlie bragge) the Churche of God, but manie rather moste
playnlie prouinge them to be the verie
Synagoge of Satan, and liuelie mem-
bers

bers of Antichriste. Yf then this, whiche seemed the true Churche of God, ād auctorised by him, so shamefullie erred: maruel it is that the papisticall Synagoge and members of Satan shuld be founde establishers of the veritie, which always since they haue bene raysed vp from hell, haue soght nothing but the vtter subuersion therof? Nether can they defende them selues by anie aucto ritie to assemble, or by anie learninge, or outwarde shewe of holynesse: seig in none of these poyntes they may be compared to this assemble, wher of S. Luke maketh métion. For here was the highe Prieste Annas, herewas Caiaphas, here were the temporal Magistrates, the gouuerners of the Temple, the Seniors of Ierusalem, the learned Scribes, and Pharisies. And what coulde anie man wishe fore in the iudgment of man, that there was not, to make a lawfull Concil? And yet thou seest the counclusion was agaynst the Lorde ād his anoynted Sóne. Wilt thou then hope for anie better at the papistes assembles and Concils, who in persecuting Christe conti-

The locusts which came out of the bottōles pit.

b. iiii.

nuallie, and his holie worde, shewe
them selues open enemies to bothe?
Doest thou here beholde the Iewes, whi
che professed the true liuinge God,
without all apishe maumetrie and I-
dolls, forbidden in their Lawe: neuerthelesse malitiouslie to consulte agaynste their true Messias: and will not yet
cease to credit the papistes, sayng,
That their Churches and Concils can

The papi-
stes are
more wic-
ked then
Iewes.

not erre, where as they dishonor the liuinge Lorde, hauing their Temples replenished with all kinde of idolatrie:
yea, when their owne consciences do
condemne them, that there was neuer
the like impietie committed in all Israel, as their filthie Concils haue taught
and commended? But thou wilt say
perchaunce, that there is no côparison
betwixt the Iewes, playnelie denying
Christ, and the papistes whiche do con-

The papi-
stes denye
Christ, as
well as
the Iewes
do.

fesse him: and therupon wilt conclude,
that the papistical Concils may not so
easilie erre, as those whiche were holdé
of the Iewes at Ierusalem, againste the
Apostels and their doctrine. As concerninge their Concils, I may not answere
                                    now

now: for that were an infinite worke to
repeate all their abſurdities. Yf any mā
wolde but once reade them ouer, he
ſholde nede no other perſuaſion to abhorre them, and to cōfeſſe this my ſay-
ing moſt true in all the Concils holden
by the Romiſhe Antichriſte. But to cō-
pare them with the Iewes in denying
of Chriſte, thou ſhalt proue them more
blaſphemous. For the Iewes after a ſorte did cōfeſſe theirChriſt and Meſſias in
wayting for him dayly to delyuer them,
and ſaue them from the miſerie wherin
they were, and now are, ād from al their
enimies accordinge as God promiſed:
but when they wolde not acknolledge
him, whom their fathers did perſecute
and crucifie, and whom the Apoſtels
taught to be riſen and aſcended, they
playnlie denied Chriſte. They beleued
that he ſhulde be their Captayne and
delyuerer, but after an other ſorte, then
by his deathe and paſſion: and to an o-
ther ende, then to ſuffer in this worlde
the ſhame of the Croſſe.

    Euenſo do the papiſtes confeſſe
Chriſte, but in effecte withe the Iewes

*The papi-
ſtes are
more blaſ-
phemous
then the
Iewes.*

The papi-
stes cófesse
Chrijt, but
in effect
deny him.

deny him. They confesse Christe whiche is come in the fleshe, borne of the virgin Marie, crucified for the synnes of the worlde, &c. Whiche all hitherunto is wel, and agreethe with vs. But for as muche as they are not with him contented, but wil haue an other Christe besides him: they are manifest de-

1.Tim. 2

niers of Christe. For (as writethe the Apostle!) There is but one God, one Mediator betwixt God and man, the man Iesus Christe, whiche gaue him selfe to be the redemption for all. Now when the papistes beleue not onlie in this

The papi-
stes cófesse
Christe to
be here in
the world
in the for-
me of bread
a dead God
not able to
do anye
thinge.

Christe and Sauiour, which came in the fleshe, and was borne of the virgine, but also in that Christe, whom they imagine to come, and to be in the worlde in the forme of bread, and borne aboute with the handes of man, not able to go him selfe: when they beleue not onelie vpon Christe crucified, and hanged vpon the Crosse, but in the coniured Idoll, hanging by a corde ouer the alter: not onlie in Christe glorified vpon the right hande of the father, who liuethe and reignethe for euer, but in

their

their rownde cake, which (they say) is consecrated, when with out sense and feeling it lieth closed in their box, subiecte to mowleinge, wormes, and corruption, reserued & kept to be worshipped as their God, but to their condemnation for euer.   More ouer when they haue other aduocates then Christe, other sacrifices for synne, other merites and means of saluation: it helpethe them no more to proue that they are Christians, thus impudentlie denying him and his office, then it helpeth the Iewes, in saying they beleue in the true Messias to come, which is all readie come, and reueled to the world.   Ye so muche the more is their condemnation, for that vnder the Name of Christe, whom they dare not deny, they worke preuie treason agaynste him, to subuerte the truethe of his Gospel, and whole fruite of his death and passion: which is our redemption from death, and hope of euerlasting life, purchased by that perfecte oblation, which was offred once for all, as a sufficient sacrifice for the synnes of the

The bony mowly. wormy, musty rotten and corrupted Christe.

The papistes vnder the name of Christians worke treason agaynst Christ.

Hebr. 10. 1.Ioh.2.

the whole worlde.

CHAP. III.

¶ *What inconueniente had commē to the Churche*
of God, if the Apostels had obeyed the commande
ment of the Concil, and what euills haue com-
men lately vpon Englande through the prea-
ching of vnlawful obediēce and yeldinge to vn-
godly Rulers.

The infi-
nit slaugh-
ter of
martyrs in
Englande.

Et vs leaue the vngodlie
papistes with their wi-
cked decrees and Con-
cils, as mē that passe the
Iewes in all maner of
wilful stubbernesse and
cruel persecution of the trueth, as the
horrible slaghter of thousandes of
martyrs, which with in these few yeres
in Englande alone do witnesse: and returne to the Apostels, Peter and Iohn,
to examine what answere they framed
to these men of auctoritie, and Rulers,
gathered to gether of all sortes, as you
haue harde, as wel of the Cleargie as of
the Laitie, of suche as thē had the onlie
gouernement of Ierusalem vnder the
Romayns, to whom they were then tri-
butaries,

butaries, which charge and threatning
of the whole Concil, done with so great aduisement and consultation, oght
not lightlie to be estemed, especiallie,
of the seruantes of God, and their sub- *We must*
iects, as the Apostels then were. They *not yelde*
were charged and threatned to preache *in Gods*
no more in the Name of Christe cruci- *cause,*
fied. An heauy commandement dout- *when man*
lesse to Peter and Iohn, especiallie if it *threat-*
might haue taken place: seing it was all *neth.*
together contrarie to their vocation
and charge geuen vnto them by their
maister Christ, to preache his Gospell
throughout all the worlde, and to be-
gyn at Ierusalem, for which cause they *Luk. 24.*
were called and chosen from amongest *act. 1.*
all others, and had bene of longe tyme
instructed of their maister Christ in the
knowledge of all his holie Scriptures,
ãd replenished with wonderful giftes of
the holie Goste, to cure all deseases, to
cast out diuels, to drinke poyson, to tre-
ad vpon serpentes, and to distribute the
holye Spirit, and all those to be as it were seales and côfirmatiõs of their doctrine, whiche all had bene to no porpose,
yf this commandement and threatninge

of the Magistrats shuld haue bene o-
beyed, & the Apostels yelded to their
auctoritie. Then the foundation of the
Churche shuld haue ben shaken, and
the whole assemble discouraged : for
the two Chief Captayns gyuinge ouer,
who durste haue presumed further?

And truelie, if the Apostels at that
tyme had bene no further instructed,
then the moste parte of men are in these our dayes, and especiallie haue bene,
and yet be in our miserable countrie
of Englande : they would haue bene in
great perplexitie, and sore afrayde to
haue made this, or the like answere
sayng : Iudge you whither it be lawful
before God to obeye you, rather then
God.   For the moste parte of men, yea
and of those whiche haue bene both
learned and godlie, and haue geuen
worthie testymonie of their profession
to the glorie of God : haue thoght and
taught (by the permission of God for
our synnes) that it was not lawful in anie
case to resist and disobeye the superior
powers: but rather to laye downe their
heades, and submitte them selues to all
kindes of punishmentes and tyrannye,
thin-

Relenting of the ministers moste dangerous.

We maye safely folowe the example of the Apostels aproued by the holy Gost.

A dangerous doctrine.

thinkinge them selues sufficientlie discharged before God of their vocation and duetie, hauing onlie the commandement of the superiour power to the contrarie, were it neuer so vngodlie ãd cleãe againste all natural reason: wherby manye hauinge commandement to preache no more Iesus christ to the people, without anie trouble of conscience haue keapt silence, and thought thé selues sufficientlie discharged: nether cõsidering that they were made stewards of Godes holye mysteries, and that not at the appointment of man, or for them selues, but by the ordinãce of our Sauiour Christ Iesus, and to be faithful distributers to others. Nether yet markinge this present answere of Peter and Iohn, whom they might safely haue folowed with better assurance: who in suche case, haue lefte this lesson for all men, rather to obaye God then mã. Others, hearinge the Name of God blasphemed by the false doctrine of the wicked and shaueling priestes, durste not once open their mouthes to speak one worde in their maisters behalff and his infallible truethe: but stopt

1. Cor. 3 Man cannot dispẽce with thatwhich God commandeth.

False brethern which betray God and his trueth in yelding to the papists.

theyr mouthes as dóme dogges, áð durste not barke against the rauenige wolff
when they knew and saw him cóming.
Many not minding to obiecte them selues to anie daunger, regardinge more
their owne safetie, then the preseruatió
of their flocke, wolde not abide the
wilde beaste commyng, but moste shamefullie fledde before the daunger came, shewing them selues playne hire-
lings, and no true pastores: leauinge the
selie shepe of God to be deuoured, and
that because they had entred in to the
folde before to feede of the flocke, to
eate the fleshe, and deuoure the people
of God as bread, rather then to do their
dueties.

No mini-
ster oght to
flie and for
sake his flo
cke, except
he be perse
cuted one-
ly, and not
his flocke.

Psal.14.

But all these and suche like are here
condemned and conuicted of euel,
which fearing man more then God, gaue eare and obedience to man, rather
then to God. Wherof, besides the iuste shame that came vpon them selues,
and the displeasure of God powred ge-
nerally vpon all (for as muche as we all
were betrayers of our maister, thoghe
not all a like) iust occasion of offence
and of like disobediéce to God, was ministred

They whi
ch please
man ra-
ther then
obey God.

niſtred to all ſorts of men , of what vocation ſo euer they were. For when they
ſawe the teachers and leaders of others
to ſet vp obedience of man rather
then of God , and the ſame confirmed
by their owne example : thoſe whiche
knewe no other, thoght it their parte
to do the like alſo in their vocation
and office.   And ſuche as were playne enimies to God, the wicked papiſtes
or diſſolute perſons, laughed in their
ſleues : ſeing bothe them and their wicked proceedings therby promoted
and furthered.   Where as to defend
their kyngdome of darckenes, ambitiō
and idle belies, there is no kyng ſo godly , no contrey ſo peaceable , nor no
kyngdome ſo ſtronge , which through
their deuiliſhe entrepriſes and wicked
perſuaſions, they haue not ſtudyed vtterly to ſubuert and deſtroy. As the example of that deſperat Moncke, who to
poiſon king Iohn, wittingly and willingly poyſoned him ſelf.   O malicious
deuil. Likewiſe the oration of that moſte traiterous and peſtilent Cardinal
Pole, doth yet witenes to all the papiſts
ſhame and confuſion : wherin he goeth

we muſt obey the preachers onely whē they bring Gods word.

The papiſtes laughe in their ſleues, when they ſee their wicked proceadinges promoted by vnlawfull obedience.

A moncke

Cardinal Pole.

c.

about to perſwade the wicked Emperour
rather to tourne his power ād armie a-
gaiſt Kynge Héry the eight ād Englād,
this doggs owne cótrey, thé againſt the
infidels, Turckes, and Sarracenes: blaſ-
phemouſlie termīg the worde ofGod ād
Goſpel of ſaluation to be the Turckeſh
ſede. O impudét mouth:ô blaſphemous
beaſt,which ſaiſt in thi heart,Ther is no
God. And yet to all your ſhame ād vtter
deſtructió of your cótrie, you haue receaued him as a God, whome before in
your lawful kyngs dayes,you moſte iu-
ſtely condemned as a traitour and very
ſonne of Antichriſt. The Counſellers,
whoſe office is to brydle the affectiós of
their Princes ād Gouuernours, in geuíg
ſuch counſele as might promote the glo
rie of God, ād the welthe of their cótrie
by this perſuaſion of obediéce,haue hitherto ſought, and yet apearinglie do,
how to accóplíſhe and ſatiſfie the vngodly luſtes of their vngodlie ād vnlaw
ful Gouerneſſe,wicked Ieſabel:who for
our ſynnes, contrarie to nature and the
manyfeſte worde of God, is ſuffred to
raigne ouer vs in Goddes furie, ād haue
therby moſte wickedlie betrayed Chriſte,their countrie,and thé ſelues (ſo mu

che as lieth in thé) to become flaues to
a ftrange and foren nation, the prowde
Spaniards. The Nobles alfo, which(tho
ghe vnworthilie wil be fo called) hea-
ring no other preaching, but that they
muft obeye their Prince, neither knowing whó, wherin, nor howfarre, haue in
like maner, as men difguifed vpon a fta
ge, turned their nobilite to open fhame
amongeft all nations, whiche now beholde their follie, and wóder ther at: feinge they are made inftrumétes of impietie, and deftroyers of their natiue
countrie, which firfte were ordayned in
Realmes to ftande in defence of trewe
religion, lawes, and welth of their nation, and to be a fhylde(to their power)
agaynft their enimies in tyme of warre,
and a brydel at home to their Princes in
tyme of peace: neither to fuffer them in
this forte to rage agaynft God, and vtterlie to conteme the holfome lawes of
the Realme, to fatisfie their filthie lufte
and vayne glorie, nor fo cruelie to mur
ther, and agaynft nature to deuoure the
people of God, their fubiects, whom
they are charged by their office to fuc-
coure and defende, and haue therfore a

*To obey is
good. but
whome,
wherin, ãd
howe far-
re, ought to
be cõsidered*

c. ii.

feareful compt to make for donige the contrarie.

The iuſti.
ces&other
vnder offi-
cers.

The Iuſtices likewiſe in Townes and Cities, as Maieres, Shryffs, Baylyfes, Conſtables, Iealers and all ſuche inferior officers, folowing the ſame exſample of vnlawful obedience, whoſe office and charge it is to miniſter iuſtice

Officers ãd
Iudges de
generat.

whithout reſpecte of perſõs, to defendè the ſymple and innocét, and to puniſhe all tranſgreſſors and malefactors, blaſphemours of Goddes holie Name, violent oppreſſers of innocentes, as be the bloudthurſtie papiſtes : are nowe become miniſters of iniuſtice, and tyranny, made tormentours of their owne naturall Countrye men, moſt blouddie butchers of their brethren, and mercileſſe murtherers of the childré of God: and that in ſuche cruel ſorte, as neuer was hearde of before ſince the deathe of Chriſte, where anie profeſſion of his Name hathe bene. In ſo muche that they are made a ſpectacle and gaſingeſtock to all countries and nations, amongeſt whom is anie feare of God or ciuile policie, whiche woulde not haue beleued it to be poſſible, if their eares

and

and eyes were not this day sufficient
wittnesses. For to vnderstand that the
papistes were cruell butchers and vn-
satiable bloudsuckers, had bene no
newes at all, they haue bene such from
the beginninge. But when they bothe
heare and see those that professe the
Gospel, and woulde be counted Christes shepe, turned for feare of displeasure, or losinge of their office in to the
nature of bloudthurstie woulues, to execute agaynst God and their conscience, the vngodlie commandementes of
the papistes: to be at commandement,
not onlie to their vnlawful Quene, but
also to euery shauen Sir Iohn, to im-
brue their handes with them in innocent bloude: this makethe all men to
wonder and be astonished.

To conclude, the residue of the comon people, seing their superiours of all
degrees ād estates, by whom they shulde be gouerned with godlie lawes, and
to whom they ought obedience in the
feare of God onelie, thus couardly to
forsake their obedience to God, and vtterlie contemne the office wherwith he
had charged them, to satisfie the vnlaw

The papistes natu-rally thurst for bloud.

Fals Gospelers, slaues vnto papistes.

The cōmon people.

ful commandements of their wilful Go-
uernesse:thinke it in no case their parte
to deny to her like obedience:but with
bodies and goodes, at home ād abrode,
to fulfill and mayntayne her will ād tyranny , not withstandinge their owne
conscience doth condemne thē,and the
worde of God dothe playnelie testifie,
that it is euell and vngodlie which they
are commanded to do. Being deceaued
by misunderstanding this place of Paule and such like:It behoueth euery soule to be subiecte to superior powers,
because there is no power but of God.
For the powers that are , be ordinances
of God: ād therfore he that resisteth the
power,resisteth the ordinaunce of God.

But how litle this and other like obi-
ectiōs make for their purpose,we shall
God willinge vnderstande,after that we
haue better examined this present answere of Peter and Iohn:who are not cō
trarie to Paul,nor Paul to them,rightly
cōsidered.For thoghe this answere was
made of Peter ād Iohn in their owne cau
se to the Magiestrates ād Rulers of Ieru
salem:yet is it no lesse generall then the
saynge of.S.Paule:and partayneth to al
conditions

Men that
do against
their con-
science and
Godes
worde.

Rom. 13.

ditions of men, as wel Magiestrates and Rulers, as inferior persons and subiectes : teaching them bothe their office moste rightlie: the one, what to commande, and how to rule : the other, whom to obeye, and wherin to be subiecte, as in their places folowinge shall euidentlie appeare.

CHAP. IIII.

The trueth of his answere was so sensible, that the verie aduersaries coulde not withstand it.

Nd firste to returne to the answere, we may be assured that it is certayne ad an vndouted true the, that in all things, and of all men, ad in all places, God is to be obeyed before mē. In so muche as the Apostels were not afrayed to cōmite the iudgement therof vnto their extreame enemies : whom they knewe right well, would haue geuen contrarie sentence, if their answere had not bene withe out all controuersie. As thoghe they would haue sayed. After that we haue bene

The enemies of God cā not denye this answere to be trewe.

c. iiii.

charged with this office to preache to
all people and nations, ād that by God
him felffe, to whom all powers are fubiecte, and all men are bownd to obeye,
whofe iudgementes none can efcape,
and whofe wrathe no flefhe is able to
abyde: whiche with the breathe of his
mouthe, moueth the heauens, and makethe the mightie mountaynes to fha-
ke and tremble, and dryueth all powers (be they neuer fo ftronge) to duft ād
powder. We are contēted to make you
iudges, which charge vs to the contrarie: whither this dreadful God may approue our doings in obeyége you beīg
men, and his creatures, yea earthe, verie duft and affhes in comparifon of his
Maieftie? Whither man, of what auctoritie fo euer he be, is able to difcharge
vs in the prefence of oure God, if in
holding our peace at your commandement, we tranfgreffe the expreffe com-
mandemét of God? That is, not to preache Iefus Chrift crucified: who hathe
chofé vs to the fame éd, indued vs with
knowledge, reuealed vnto vs his fecret
counfels, the myfterie of our redemption, and armed vs with all giftes
of

Pfal. 104.

*Preachers
muft prea-
ch Chrifte
in feafon
and out of
feafon.*

of the holie Goſt , neceſſarie for the
accompliſhement of ſo waightie an
entrepriſe .   We nede not herein to
vſe many wordes or reaſons : nor to
deſier anie arbiters to define this matter : be you your ſelues iudges . Which
kinde of ſpeaking, men commonlie vſe,
when the matter is euident and out of
doubte , knowen to all men , be they of
neuer ſo ſlender iudgement , and nede
no further reaſons, or Scriptures to proue it. The like kinde of reaſoninge, the
Apoſtle vſeth agaynſt the Corinthians: I. Cor. II.
who permitted their wemé to praye bareheaded in the Congregation , which
he condemned as an vndecent cuſtome,
not becommyng the Saynɛts of God.
For amongeſt other reaſons, he likewiſe makethe them ſelues iudges in the
matter, ſayeng: Iudge ye amonge your
ſelues, whither it be cumlie for a womã
to praye bareheaded in the Congregation. Cócludinge, that verie nature dothe teache the contrarye. In like maner
this anſwere is ſo true and ſenſible (that
rather God is to be obeyed then man)
that there cã be none ſo malitious or ig
norante , whom verie nature will not

compel to confeſſe it, if he had no further knowledge. Nether had theſe men,
for all their great a doo, lóge conſulta-
cion, hie learninge and wiſdome (deſie-
rous alſo to take occaſion agaynſt the
Apoſtels) anie thinge to ſaye for the cótrary. But as Gods enemies are accuſtomed, when their mouthes are ſtopt,
either with raylinges, or threatnings,
to expreſſe their rage: ſo did they with
Peter & Iohn, dimitting them at the laſt
with bitter wordes and menaces: and
they departed notwithſtandinge from
the Concile, by the means of this anſwe
re, conquerours.

They ſhuld not ſo haue eſcaped if they had bene befor our cruell Counſelors Phariſies and Hypocrits of Englande.

CHAP. V.

¶ *To obeye man in anie thinge agaynſt God, is Vn-lawfull in d playne diſobedience.*

what things are to be conſidered.

Now for as muche as we a
re aſſured of the trueth
ád certantie of their anſ
were, wherof none can
iuſtlie doute: let vs ſo-
mewhat further conſi-
der what thinges are pricipallie here in
conteyned. Firſt we maye hereof iuſtlie
conclude, that to obeye man in anie
thinge contrary to God, or his precepts
thoghe he be in hieſt auctoritie, or ne-

uer so orderly called there vnto (as these men, wherof Luke speaketh, were) is
no obedience at all, but disobedience.

Secondlie, that it is not a sufficient
discharge for vs before God, whé we de
nye to accóplyshe their vnlawful demá
des and threatnings, except we do the
cótrarie euery man in his vocation and
office, as occasion is offred, and as his
power will serue. Whiche thiges playnlie vnderstáde, as they shal geue a clere
light in this controuersie : so do I not
doute by this present answere and facte
of Peter and Iohn, to proue moste mani
festlie, that althoghe we were destitute
of other examples, yet this might appea
re sufficient. As touchinge the firste,
that there is no obedience agaynst God
which is not playne disobedience : the
Apostles say, Iudge you whither it be ri
ght or iust in Godds sight to obeye you
rather théGod: which is as muche as thei
would saye, It is not iuste nor lawful.
Thé if it be not lawful and iust in Goddes sight, who iudgeth things truelie ád
as thei be in dede, it must nedes folowe
that allmaner of obediéce agaynst God
ád his worde, is playne disobediéce, and

Obedien-
ce agaynst
God is dis-
obedience,

the workers therof likewise condemn-
ned as rebells. Why? Bycause it is vniust
and vnlawfull before God: And all true
obedience is lawful, which must not be
measured by the will of mã, but by the
iuste Lawes and ordinances of the liuin
ge Lorde.   So that after God hathe
once pronounced anie thinge that he
would haue done, either in his Lawe or
otherwise: there is no man that may or
can dispence therwith, seeme it of neuer
so litle importance in the iudgement
of men.   He that commandeth the
contrarie, is a rebell: and he that obey-
eth likewise. Neither dothe this appertayne to the Apostles and ministers onlie in their office, but is a generall argument for all sortes, estates, and degrees
of men: for as muche as God hathe like
auctoritie of all, and all owe vnto him
first and principall obedience: and secondly vnto men for him, and in him on
lie: except they wil be enimies to God,
and deny him to be their Lorde. For so
muche it is in effecte, when we preferre
men to God, obedience to man, before
the obedience to God. It is not the auctoritie of the Prince, or the feare of his
punish-

what God
once wil-
lith in his
Law to be
done or not
to be done
that cã no
man dis-
pence wi-
th be it ne-
uer so smal
in the sight
of man.

punifhmēt, that cā excuse in his prefence: who cōmādeth his people generalie, **Deu. 4.**
high and lowe, riche and poore, man ād
womā, to heare his voyce, and to obferue his ftatutes. Nether to declyne vpon
the right hand, nor vpon the lefte : nether to adde anie thinge therto, or to ta
ke anie thinge from it : but to do that
onlie, whiche the liuinge Lorde commā
deth. And if we be the fhepe of the Lordes foulde, it is not fufficiét forvs to hea
re the voyce of our paftor, ād to folowe
him, except we alfo deny to heare, muche more to folowe anie other : that is,
which calleth not with the voyce of **Ioh. 10.**
the true paftor. And as there ought to
be no creature of like auctoritie amongeft vs, as our foueraygne Lorde and
God, whofe creatures we be, and the
workemanfhip of his owne hādes : euen
fo, there is none like to him in dignitie,
or may be cōpared to him in power, no
ne like to him in riches, or fo able to
rewarde his fubiectes, beinge Lorde of
heauē and earthe, difpofer of all things
prefent and to come: diftributer not
onlie of all corporall and earthlie blef-
fings to thofe that feare and ferue him:

but alfo powreth vpon them all fpi-
tuall and heauenlie graces in great a-
boundance. Moreouer, as by his auctori
tie, power, dignitie, riches and liberali-
tie, he maye of right demande of vs obe
dience : fo muft we perfuade our felues
in not rédring the fame to him willing-
lie, that none câ deliuer vs from his hor
rible punifhementes and deftruction,
whiche he threatneth vpon all fuch as
wilfully trangreffe his holie preceptes,
âd declyne from his Lawes. Nether wil
he regarde by what means, or by whofe
cômandement we tranfgreffe his lawes.
For that can be no excufe for vs, thoghe
he be Kinge, Quene, or Emperour that
commandeth or threatneth vs . For
what is kinge, Quene, or Emperour
compared to God? Is the punifhement
of earthe, afhes, of vile man, whofe bre-
ath is in his noftrilles, more to be feared then the plages of God, who hath
power both of body and foule to deftroye thé euerlaftingly? Was it any earthly power that broght the waters vpon
the vniuerfall worlde, and drowned all
mankinde for fynne, viii perfons excep
ted? Did man deftroye Sodome and Go-
morrhe

Deu. 28, and. 30. No cóman dem•nt fhall excufe vs in the daye of vengeance.

Efai. 2.

Gen. 7

morrhe with fier and brymſtone? Came
the plages of Egypt, the drowninge of
Pharao, the ouertrow of the Cananites,
the ſubuerſion of Ieruſalem, by the
power of man? If theſe be the workes
of man and not of God, feare man and
not God : but if there be none of
theſe euells which cometh vpon a-
nie Citie, or contrie, wherof the Lorde is not the worker: beware that the
feare of mans puniſhment, cauſe thee
not to fall in to the handes of this migh
tie reuéger, whiche is an horrible thinge, as the Apoſtle writeth.   Princes
therfore, and all powers vpon thee arth,
are not to be compared vnto God, whoſe Lieutenants onlie they ſhuld be, and
are no longer then he wil, in whoſe han
des their hartes are, to moue and turne
at his pleaſure. And for that cauſe it is
their duetie to ſeke all means poſſible,
wherbie the glorie of God might be ad-
uanced, by whom they are them ſelues
ſo highlie exalted aboue their brethern, and in no cauſe to miniſter occaſion of rebellion agaynſt his mightie
Maieſtie: but rather to be examples to
others (ouer whom they are conſtitute)
of all Godlie liffe and lawfull obe-

Gen. 14.
Exod. 3 4.
5. 6. 14.

Amos 3.

Heb. 13.

Pro. 21.

dience. In consideration wherof, God
him selfe appoyntig his people to haue
a kinge, which, when they shulde come
in to the lande of promeste (for that was
the first promotion that God ordeyned
amongest his people, which yet came
not to suche pride to desire an Emperour) did with great circumspection, as
well appoynt them what maner of man
they shulde chose, as the lawes by the
whiche he shuld rule others, and be o-
beyed of them. When thou commest
(saithe the Lorde by Moyses) to the lan
de which thy Lorde geueth thee, and
shalt possesse it, thou shalt with out dou
te, put or constitute a kinge to thee: but
who thy Lorde thy God shall chose.
Moreouer he saith, from the middle of
thy brethern shalt thow appoynt a Kíge
ouer thee. For thou mayst not appoynt
a stráger, which is not thy brother. Which lawe, as it proceaded from the wisedome of God, who thoght it necessarie
for his people: euen so is our miserable
ignorance and vnspeakeable ingratitude to be lamented, which nether do vnderstand the goodnesse of God in these
lawes, not yet will vouchesaffe to con-
sult

what ma-
ner of man
the Lorde
woulde
haue cho -
sen kinge.
Deut. 17.

sult with his heauély wisedome: all men
rather sckinge to chose and procure
them selues Princes and kinges after
their owne phātasie, ād by vngodlie fetches and policies, then to folowe the ap
poyntment of the Almightie: preferringe theyr owne wittes to the wisedome
of God, whiche neuer fayleth them that
folowe it. In comparison of whom all o-
thers at lengh, shall shewe them selues
to be meere fooles. Yf we wilbe the peo
ple of God, let vs then searche and diligentlie folowe the Lawes of God, especiallie in so weightie matters, as the e-
lection of kinges and Princes, by whom
Realmes and nations are either preserued if they be Godlie, or vtterly di-
stroyed, and shamefullie oppressed if
they be vngodlie. The first poynt or
cautiō that God requireth of his people
to obserue, is, that they chose suche a
kinge, as the Lorde dothe appoynt, and
not as they phantasie. And what one is
he or how shuld he be knowé? The peo
ple of Israel (you will saie) had their kīges appoynted them by the mouthe of
God and anoynted of his Prophets: as
d.

Gods La-
wes must
diligentlie
be folowed
in election
of kinges
ād Rulers
and not
mans phā-
tasie.

The firste
note and
obseruatiō
in chosinge
of a kynge
Ezechi. 20

Dauid, and his sonne Salomon. For Saule, thoghe he was appoynted ād anoye-
ted in Goddes furie, yet was he not
of the Lordes chosinge after this meaning of Moyses, who willethe them to
appoynte a kinge that the Lorde shal
chose: to wit, of his fauour and goodnesse, suche a one as shall obserue the
Two notes
to knowe
whether a
kinge be
chosen of
God or no
Lawes folowing, as we shall see here
after.   Two means had the Israelites to knowe their kinge, whither he
was of God electe or no.   The firste,
by the expresse commandement and
promesse made to some especiall man,
wherof they neded not to doute: as was
made to Dauid, ād to Salomō his sonne
expresslie.   The secōde is by his worde, which he hathe now left to all men
to be the ordinarie means to reueale
his will and appoyntment. Which (if
we vnfaynedly folowe in our doings)
we nede no more to doute, then if
God shulde now speake vnto vs out of
the heauens, as then he did to the Israelites. The worde then geueth vs
these notes to know whither he be
of God or not, whom we woulde chose
for our kinge. Firste (as was sayd) if he
be a

be a man that hathe the feare of God
before his eyes, and zeflye with Dauid, and Iofias, dothe ftudie to fet forthe the fame, hatinge vnfaynedlie al
papiftrie and idolatrie. For this caufe
God willeth that he fhuld be chofen
from amongefte his brethern, and fhulde be no ftranger: bycaufe fuche then
had not the feare of God, but were idolaters, to whom no promeffe of anie
kingdome was made, and who alfo
would leade the people to idolatrie.
Alfo in that his exercife is appoynted,
the worde, Lawes & ftatutes of God, it
is manifefte that he is not chofen of
God, except he be fuch a one: and oght
not to be anoynted or elected as their
kinge and Gouernour, what title or
right fo euer he feeme to haue theruto,
by ciuile policie, except he be a pro-
moter & fetter forthe of Godds Lawes
and glorie, for whiche caufe chieflie,
this office was ordeyned.

The nexte rule to be obferued is,
that he fhulde be one of their brethern, meaninge of the Ifraelits: part-
lie to exclude the oppreffion and
d ii.

None oght to be chofen a kinge or Ruler but fuch as wil maintaine and promote Godes Lawes. The fecõd note why-kinges ar chofen frõ amongeft their bre-thern.

idolatrie, whiche commeth in by strangers, as our Contrie now is an example:
and partlye, for that strangers cannot
beare such a natural zeale to straunge
realmes and peoples, as becomethe brethern: but chiefsie to auoyde that mon-
ster in nature, and disordre amongest
men, whiche is the Empire ād gouernement of a woman, sayinge expresslie:
From the myddle of thy brethren shalt
thou chose thee a kinge, and not amon-
gist thy sisters. For God is not contrarie
to him self, whiche at the begynninge
appoynted the woman to be in subiection to her housbande, and the man to
be head of the woman (as saithe the A-
postle) who wil not permitte so muche
to the womā, as to speake in the Assemblie of men, muchelesse to be Ruler of a
Realme or nation.　　Yf women be
not permitted by Ciuile policies to rule in inferior offices, to be Coūsellours,
Pears of a realme, Iustices, Shireffs, Bay
liues and such like: I make your selues
iudges, whither it be mete for them
to gouerne whole Realmes and natiós?
　　If the worde of God can not persuade

(marginal notes:)

The gouer-
nemẻnt of
women is
against
nature,
and Gods
ordinance.

Gen. 3.

1. Cor. 14
1. Tim. 2.

women by
ciuell poli-
ce are ex-
cluded frōe
all offices
in a comon
welth.

suade you, by which she is made subiect
to her housbande, muche more to the
Counselle and auctoritie of an whole
realme, which worde also appoynteth
your kinges to be chosen from amonge
their brethren, and not from their sisters: who are forbidden as persons vn-
mete to speake in a Congregacion: be
you your selues iudges, and let nature
teache you the absurditie therof.

And thus muche haue I of pourpose
noted in this matter, to let you see to all
our shames, how farre ye haue bene led
besydes your commun senses and the
manifest worde of God, in electing, a-
noynting, and crowninge a woman to
be your Quene ād Gouernesse, and she
in verie dede a bastarde, and vnlawfully begotten. But beit that she were no bastarde, but the kinges daughter as lawfullie begotten as was her si-
ster, that Godlie Lady, ād meke Lambe,
voyde of all Spanishe pride, and strange bloude : yet in the sicknesse, and
at the deathe of our lawfull Prince of
Godlie memorie kynge Edwarde the
sixt, this shulde not haue bene your

Winche-
ster proueth
her a
bastard in
his boke
de Vera o-
bedientia,
and Bōner
also in the
preface of
the same
boke.
kyng Ed-
ward the
VI.

firſte counſele or queſtion, who ſhulde be your Quene, what womã you ſhul
de crowne, if you had bene preferrers
of Goddes glorie, and wiſe coũſelours,
or naturallie affected towardes your
countrie. But firſte and principallie, who
had bene moſte meeteſt amengeſt your,
brethern to haue had the gouernement
ouer you, and the whole gouernement
of the realme, to rule them carefullie in

They haue now plentie of both ſortes.

the feare of God, and to preſerue them
agaynſt all oppreſsion of inwarde tyrants and outwarde enemies.   Wher
bie you might haue bene aſtured to eſ-
kape all this miſerable & vnſpeakable
diſordre, and ſhamefull confuſion, whiche now by contrarie counſele is broght worthely vpon vs.   I knowe ye
will ſaye, the Crowne is not intayled to
the heyre males onelie, but appartay-
nethe aſwel to the daughters: and ther-

The title of the Crowne belongeth onely by Gods worde, to the heyres males.

fore by the Lawes of the Realme, you
coulde not otherwiſe do. But yf it be
true, yet miſerable is this anſwere of
ſuche as had ſo longe tyme profeſſed
the Goſpel, and the lyuelie worde of
God. Yf it had bene made of pagãs and
heathens, whiche knew not God by his
worde,

worde, it might better haue bene borne with all. But amongest them that beare the Name of Godds people, with whó his Lawes fhulde haue chief auctoritie: this anfwere is not tollerable to make the conftant and vndouted Lawe of God, whiche oght to be the lyne of all ordinaunces, to geue place to the vayne and vngodlie decrees of men, as experience hath now taught you. Mo reouer, in anoynting her as iffhe had bene a man, was no leffe abfurditie, vfinge thervnto fuche greafinges ád fhá leffe Ceremonies, ád that in the face of all the people: as thoghe Moyfes lawe yet were in force, and Chrift our Sauiour not comé: which hath put an end to all fuche outwarde Ceremonies: whofe annoyntings were fpirituall . For as he was replenifhed with all graces of the holie Goft, and that with out meafure, and aboue all his felows, kings, Priefts, and Prophetes: fo hathe he left no other annoyntinge to be vfed of his feruaunts: but of the fame forte, that is, fpirituall. And yf Moyfes with his Ceremonies were now in full auctoritie, as he was before Chrifte: Yet were it

d. iiii.

Youre owne Lawes dothe not prefer a baftard to her that is lauful begotten.

Heb. I.
Pfal. 45.

not lawful by him to anoynte anie woman, to ani maner of office or dignitie,

Leuit .8.
1.Sam. 15
1.Reg. 19

seing that this Ceremonie was neuer
appoynted to anie other but onelie to
Priests, kinges, and Prophetes. How dur
ste you then be so bolde and impudent
ô Papists, (for this was your entreprise)
to transgresse the order of God in the
Lawe of Moyses by anoyntige a womā?
And also to contemne the libertie of
the Gospell, in reducinge and bringing
agayn the Iewishe Ceremonies, from
whiche by Christe we are delyuered?
But it is no maruell if you be all wa-
ies like your selues, stubberne and rebellious enimies to God and contem-
ners of Christe. And therfore leauinge
you to your selues, we will retourne to
Goddes appoynted limites in his Lawe,
for the lawfull election of kinges and
Princes.   Ye haue hearde the two firste cautions or rules, that is, how he mu
ste be of Godds appoyntment, and
not of mans · And also from amon-

The thirde
rule to be
obserued
in electing
of kinges.

gest your brethren and not of your sisters, and why. The thirde caution
that God specifieth in this election is,
that he be none such as hath great nom
ber

ber of horſes: meaning, as truſteth in
his owne power, and preparation of all
thinges, for defence of him ſelfe, ād to
ouercome his enemies. For vnder this
name of horſes, he comprehendeth all
ingeynes and furniture of warre: ſuche
a one, as truſteth in them, and makethe not God his arme and bockler, with
faitheful Dauid, is not meete to be kinge of the Lordes people.

For by ſuch means ſhulde they be
broght to Egypte agayne, to their olde
miſerie and ſlauerie, if they delited in
their horſes, from whence the Lorde
woulde haue them kepte, and not in a-
nie caſe to returne. As no doute, he
woulde haue had vs miſerable Engliſhe men, warelie to haue kepte vs in
that libertie of Ieſus Chriſte and our
conſciences, wherin ſo mercifullie he
had broght vs: and not by placeinge an
infidel woman ouer vs, to returne to
our olde vomite, muche more viler thē
the ſlauerie of Egypte, I meane the ſeruitude of that Romiſhe Antichriſte.

Other obſeruations he geueth alſo,
not to ſeke manie wiues, nor to heape
vp muche golde: but chiſlie that he ha-

Pſal. 52.

*What o-
ther notes
God geueth
to choſe by.*

ue an example of Goddes Lawes prescri
bed vnto him, to reade in them all the
dayes of his life, that he maye learne
to feare the Lorde and to keepe his cō-
mandements, and not to lifte him self
vp aboue his brethren: meaning, he
shulde rule with all holynesse and hum
blenesse, as did Moyses and Dauid. And
therby, dothe God promisse that his dayes, and the dayes of his children shall
be prolonged in the middle of Israell.

Of the whiche we may iustlie conclude, that by the ordinance of God, no o-
ther kinges or Rulers, oght to be chosen to rule ouer vs, but suche as will seeke his honor and glorie, and will com
maunde and do nothing contrarie to
his Lawe. Wherewith they are no lesse,
ye muche more charged, then the common people: becaufe their charge is
double: that is, not onelie to feare God
them selues, but to see that their people feare him also, to whom they owe
in that case all humble obedience and
reuerence. For they be (as was sayed)
Goddes subiectes and Lieutenantes, for
whose cause they must be reuerenced,
doinge their duetie.   But if they will
abufe

As the kings charge is greater, so is he more bonde to God to performe the same.

abuſe his power, liſtinge them ſelues a-
boue God and aboue their brethren, to
drawe them to idolatrie, and to oppreſſe them, and their contrie: then are they
nomore to be obeyed in any commandements tending to that ende: but to
be cōtemned as vile Sergeantes in com
pariſon of the high Iudge and Magiſtrate, who oght to do nothing, but as
he is commaunded to do by the Iudge
ād ſuperior power according to the lawe. Other wiſe, if he liſt him ſelfe aboue the chief Iudge, lokyng to be honored and obeyed more then he: who
would not abhorre ſuche a Sergeant, ād
not onelie to withſtande his cōmandement, but to accuſe him as a rebellious
traytor, and baniſhe him from a mon-
geſt them?   And yet here is but rebellion agaynſt man, who is but mortall.
What oght we thē to do vnto that kinge or Prince, that liſteth him ſelfe vp
agaynſt the Maieſtie of God, who is im-
mortal, to whome belongeth all power,
dominion and honor? Is he anie more in
compariſon of God, then the Sergeant
in reſpecte of the Iudge? Shall the Sergeant be puniſhed as a traytor, and this
man honored as a kinge, which doth no

If it be hey nous to diſobey mā, much more God the Lorde of al thinges.

parte of the office therunto belonginge? Or rather is not his crime and treason greater, and deſeruith ſo muche more, as God is more excellent, compared to anie worldlie power, then is a nie kinge or Prince compared to the moſte vileſte Sergeant?

Moreouer, whence hathe he this honor? Of him ſelfe? Is anie man naturallie borne a kinge, Or hathe he it of God? And if of God, wherto, but to vſe it with God, ãd not agaynſte him. Seing then it is not iuſte in Goddes ſight to obeye man rather then God: neither *Kinges* that their is anie diſpenſacion of man *oght to ru* that cã diſpéce with his holie cõmande *le in Gods* ments, neither the auctoritie of Prin- *feare with,* ce, nor feare of puniſhment can excuſe *him ãd not* vs. Seing alſo, that kinges are inſtitute *againſte* to rule in Goddes feare and Lawes, as *him.* ſubiectes and Sergeants to God, and *To obey a* not agaynſte his Lawes, and aboue him: *wicked* it muſte nedes followe (as we firſte ſay- *Prince in* ed) that all obedience geuen to ſuche, *his wic-* wicked Princes agaynſte God, is play- *kednes is* ne rebellion in his iudgemente. And in *plaine diſ-* that caſe to obeye God, and diſobeye *obedience* man, is true obedience, how ſo euer the *to God.* worlde

worlde iudgeth . For as none will condemne Peter and Iohn of difobedien-
ce, becaufe they woulde not herein o-
beye their ordynarie Magiftrates : nomore will anie which haue right iudgement , condemne the like refiftance in
others, which alike is lawfull to all.

Or ells fhulde the Ifraelites be excu- I.king.I.
fed, by caufe they obeyed their wicked
kinge Ieroboam in worfhippinge his
calues in Dan, and Bethel.

Then fhuld that cruell butcher Doeg, I.Sam. 22
in killinge Ahimalech with LXXXV Priefts or Leuites, and the whole towne of
Nob , at the commandement of vngodlie kinge Saul , haue bene preferred
to the refte of all his feruantes and foul Mat.2.
diars.   And the fouldiars alfo of cruell *They will*
Herode fhuld be blameleffe in murthe- *make*
rig ãd fheading the bloude of fo many *all thefe*
infantes in Bethlehem at Herods com- *blãles (the*
mandement .   Then fhulde the wicked *papiftes are*
Iewes be gyltleffe of Chriftes deathe ãd *oimpudẽt)*
his Prophets , whom they confented to *rather thẽ*
murther by the parfuafion of their Ru- *they will*
lers. And the counterfayte Chriftians *feme to*
this day, which euerie where (but efpe- *offende.*
ciallie in our miferable countrie) im- *Mat. 27.*

prifon, famifhe, murther, hange, and
burne their owne countriemen, and dea
re children of God, at the commandement of furious Iefabel, and her falfe
Prieftes and Prophetes, the blouddie
Bifhopps and fhauelynges, fhulde be
giltleffe in all their doinges. But all thefe doth God (who is a Ielious ād righ-
teous God, and cannot abide his honor
to be geuen to any other, nor fuffer the
bloude of the innocent longe to crie
vnto him for vengeance) condemne as
blafphemers, idolatres, and cruell murtherers: which faithe: Thou fhalt haue
no other Goddes but me. Thou fhalt rot
kill. And if God dothe make this, difo-
bedience (as thou mayft playnely fee)
what commandement of man can aul-
ter his fentence, before whom there is
no obedience in euil thinges? Yea, if the
whole multitude, from the hieft to the
loweft, wolde agree and confent to do
euel, yet mufte not thou followe them
faith the Lorde. For if thou do (notwith-
ftanding the commandement of thy
Prince, or example of all others) thou
art with them a rebell, and a rebell a-
gaynft thy Lorde and God: from whofe
wrathe

Exod. 20.
Pfalm 9.
Gen. 4.

The com-
mandemēt
of the Prin
ce fhall not
excufe thee
in euill
doyng.

wrathe and heauie indignation, no man can defende thee in the dreadfull daie of his visitacion, which is at hande.

CHAP. VI.

How it is not inough to denye wicked commandeméts of all kinde of Rulers, except we withstand them also, euery man according to his vocation, in doing the contrary.

AS by this answere afore mentioned, we haue bene taught not to geue place to the vnlawfull commandemétes of Magistrates, in what auctoritie so euer they be, because it is nothing but rebellion in the iudgement of God: euen so may we learne by the same answere and example of the Apostles, how God requiereth more at our handes, that is, to withstande their preceptes, in doing the contrary: euery man according to his office and estate wherin God hathe placed him. For as man thinketh him self not fullie

It is not inoughe not to do the wicked commaundement of a kynge, but also to do the contrarie.

obeyed, when we abftayne from thofe
thinges which he forbiddeth, except
moreouer we do the contrary, which
he commandeth: euenfo may we muche more thinke, that God is not fullie
obeyed, when we will not do the vngodlie commandements of men, except
alfo we applye our felues with all diligence to do the contrary. So did Peter
and Iohn make anfwere, denying to do
as they were comaunded by the Magiftrates. And as they denyed in wordes,
fo did they, ād the reft of the Apoftles in
effecte, as the courfe of the hiftorie doth
witneffe. Who went all to gether to the
Temple after they were dimiffed, and
preached openlie in the face of all the
people Iefus Chrifte crucified, not with
ftanding all the afore named threatnynges and menacinges, yea afterwarde, when they had bene imprifoned
and then by the Angel of God deliuered, and whipped mofte vilely, as if
they had bene flaues: yet were they nothing therby difcouraged, but continued in one mynde and anfwere, fayng
as they did before with one voyce and
confent: God mufte be obeyed before
man.

Act.5.

man, and boldlie preached their maister
Christ, contemning all displeasures whi
ch they for his Names sake sustened, re   *Act. 5.*
membring well his sure and consorta-
ble promesses who said: Blessed are you   *Matth. 5.*
when men reuile you and sklander you,
and speake all euill againste you, lying,
for my sake: be glad and reioce, for greate is your rewarde inthe kingdome of
heauen. For so did they persecute the
prophetes before you.

Thus see we thé, how the trueth of this
doctrine is not proued onely by the fir-
ste examination of Peter and Iohn: but   *Al the apo-*
also confirmed the second tyme by the   *stels to ge-*
rest of all the Apostels agreeinge therin,   *ther shew-*
and suffringe vile scourginge for the   *ed the*
same: not onely boldlie affirminge it in   *like con-*
the presence of all the Magistrates at Ie- *stancie.*
rusalem, but as constantly approuinge
it in their doinges: when contrarie to
their commandemétes, they ceased not
more diligentlye to publishe the doctrine of saluation: reioysinge and praysi-
nge God, who had made them worthie
to suffer for his Sónes sake, their Lorde
and maister. O worthy and manful
souldiars, O moste trustie and payne-

e.

ful seruantes: neither feringe the prowde lokes and malitious threatninges of

*No power
can preuail
against the
faithfull.*

the whole Senate and power of Ierusalem: nor shrinking in their office, for
all their cruel punishments. But the more they were forbidden, and the oftener
they were punished: the stouter, stronger,
and mightier were they to fight against their enemies with the spiritual sworde, wherwith they were charged in
their maisters quarel: beinge assured allwayes of this, that he who gaue thē auctoritie to preach, woulde geue thē stre
ngh also for the performance therof, as

Mar.28.

he had promesed, sayinge: I will be with
you to the end of the worlde. And he
beinge with thē, (as the Apostle saithe)

Rom.8.

what should they care who were against
them? A worthie example ād mirour for
all such to beholde as are called of God
to be his messengers and disposers of
his holie mysteries, how faithful they

1.Cor.4.

oght to be in the distribution of the same, omitting no maner of occasions, o-
beying no contrarie commandements,
nor fearing the cruel threatninges of
men,

God

God hath geuen them the charge of moste pretious iewels, and ineſtimable riches : not to be hid in a corner, or retayned with them ſelues : but rather (as the Apoſtle exhorteth) to ſtyrre vp the gyfte of God, which is in them, and not to neglect it, to preache the worde of God, and to be inſtant in ſeaſon and out of ſeaſon, to conuince, reproue, and exhorte with all ſoftneſſe and learning. For this is that ſharpe and two edged ſworde wherewith God hath not onely armed them agaynſte their enimies : but to fight alſo manfullie for others agaynſt all powers worldly and ſpiritual, with this mightie and ſpiritual ſworde the worde of God. *Ephe. 3.*

1. Tim. 4.

2. Tim. 4.

Ephe. 6.

Heb. 4.

For otherwiſe, if Chriſte him ſelf had ceaſed to preache his Fathers will, for which cauſe partly he was ſent in to the worlde, for feare of threatninges, conſpiracies, commandements, and puniſhments of men : where had bene this comfortable doctrine of ſaluation? When ſhulde he haue ſuffred death, for our redemption and delyuerance?

How ſhuld the Apoſtles and all

other faithfull martyrs, which by their deathes in all ages, haue geuen glorie to Chriſt, haue left behinde them ſo worthie monumentes, and comfortable writinges, beſides the notable examples of conſtancie in ſealinge vp their doct rine with the ſheading of their bloud, if they had yealded or ſhronke in executinge their office for feare of anie power. And in oure miſerable Countrie, where Antichriſt this day is againe for oure ſynnes exalted, if commandeméts of tyrantes ſhuld haue taken place in all men, as it did with many hirelinge preachers, ſome moſte ſhamefullie denying their Maiſter Chriſte, taking vpon them the marke of the beaſte, miniſtring poyſon for foode to their flocke, ſome in makinge a ſpoyle and praye of their flocke, and as cowardes takeyng them to their feete, leauing the poore lambes of God with out all comforte, to be deuoured of the wilde rauenous beaſtes: ſome alſo in playng on both partes with the halting Iſraelites, thinke to ſerue God and Baal: if in all others (I ſaie) as in theſe, the vngodlie decrees of men ſhulde haue

Chriſt diſ obeyed wicked magiſtrates and ſo ſaued vs: but we obey vniuſt magiſtrates and deſtroy our ſelues.

1. kin. 18.
2. Cor. 6.

taken

taken place : how coulde we haue had
these worthie examples of so many hun
dreth martyrs, who haue glorified Christe moste constantlie, in offringe vp their liues as amoste swete sauour to the
Lorde? And that of all sortes of men and
women, young and olde, riche and poore, learned and vnlearned, all being herein persuaded (not able perchaunce to
do anie more for the comfort of others,
in so generall a defection from God)
haue chosē rather with the losse of this
corporall lyfe, to obeye God, then o-
therwise to lyue in welthe and obeye
man . For the which, the Name of God
be praysed for euer, who styrre vp our
hartes by their examples, and prepare vs
with the grace of his holie Spirite to
the like constancie and obedience.

Obedience to death.

Besides this we learne by the cōmand-
ements of God, that so oft as he forbid
deth any thing which he wolde not to
be done , in the self same, he commandeth vs the contrarie, as for example:
Thow shalt not murther, Steale, Commit adultrie, or Beare false wittnes . It
is not ynough to abstaine frome these

When God for-biddeth onethinge he commā-deth the contrarie

e. iii.

thinges, neither is God therin fullie
obeyed, except we do the contrarie, so
oft as occasion is ministred, that is , to
saue, preserue, and defende, as well the
goodes as the persones of our brethren
and neghbours . And this is a certayne
and general rule, not onely in these examples here named : but in all other
preceptes whither they be of the Ten
commandments , or anie other besides
conteyned in the Scriptures : that what
so euer God forbiddeth anie man , in
the same he is charged to do the contrarie according to his power, thogh
all the worlde would stande agaynst
him . In confirmation wherof, let vs o-
nelie consider the notable example of
the Godlie Prophet Daniel , who when
he was commanded in the name of kinge Darius (by whome he had bene promoted to great honor, and of all other
was in best fauor, and hiest reputation
with him) to aske nothing of his God,
or anie other for the space of thirtie
dayes , but onely of Darius his kinge,
according to the decree made at the
requeste of his vngodlie counsel , pur-
poslie

Dani.6.

Daniel
was no
Englishe
courtier:
for he
coulde not
flatter.

posſie agaynſt Daniel, would not obeye
the commandement, being not ignorant that it was a publike decree, which
all (he onely excepte) obeyed.   And
alſo how death (and that moſte terri-
ble, to be caſt among the hungry lyons) was appoynted for a puniſhment
to the tranſgreſſors. But Daniel not
contented to do as he was commanded, did as he was accuſtomed, the
contrary: not once, but thriſe euery
day, tranſgreſsinge the kinges commādement, prayinge to the liuinge Lorde
his God. And to the intent it might be
knowen abrode to al men, that he contemned this vngodly commandement,
he ſet open his windowes more then cuſtome, to the itét that all whiche wolde,
might beholde his doing: ſo glad was
he to be knowen to ſerue the true and
mightie God.   Here wolde our worldly wiſe men, no dout, condemne Daniel of raſhnes and follye in doing,
more then was expedient.   What
nede he thus to prouoke the indignation of a Prince, who had power with a worde of his mouth to di-

*Note this
al ye Gen-
telmen ãd
Nobles of
Inglande*

*Daniel bu-
rned with
the zeal of
Gods glory
and wolde
not hide it*

e. iiii,

stroye him? Yf he wolde not aſke anie
thing in the Name of Darius as others

The coũſel of the wordlye diſſemblers

did, yet might he haue abſtayned from
praying to God for that ſpace. Was thir
tie dayes ſo great a matter, that he
might not abſtayne from praying to
God, to gratifie therby his Prince to
whome he was ſo muche bounde? And
if he wolde nedes praye to God, could
he not haue done it preuely and ſecret-
ly? What nede he to ſet open his win-
dow in the ſight of al men? This was an
open contempte of the kinges Maieſtie:

Carnal Goſpelers are halters õ both ſides

this was a greater offence, then the facte
it ſelf. Thus wolde the politike ãd worl-
dlinges reaſon, as our carnall Goſpellers do daylie, to mayntayne their ſha-
meles halting vpon both partes, to cloke their owne impietie, and to intice o-
thers to do the like. But faythful Daniel
had learned an other leſſon, and of a
more faithfull ſcholemaiſter: euen the
verie ſame that inſtructed here the
Apoſtles, the Spirite of God, the au-

Ioh. 16.

ctor of wiſedome, and trueth: that
he oght not onelie to contemne
the kinges vnlawfull commandement,
but

but to do the plaine contrarie . Nether thoght he it sufficient to do this secretly , except openly he shewed to all the worlde whose seruante he was, and what God he honored . Otherwise , how colde he haue declared to the people , that he loued his God with all his harte , soule and power , as was commanded?

Daniel was not so wyse as our glauering Gospellers.

CHAP. VII.

All men are bound to follow the like example , as wel as the Apostles and Daniel , of what estate and condicion so euer they be.

Ere are all excuses taken away from all men, that will be true Christians , and haue the Apostles and Daniel for their instructers and teachers: whither they be Counsellers, Nobles, Peares, or inferior and ciuile officiers . But they will peraduéture excuse them selues , as thogh God had no thing to do with thé , becaue they be not Apostels, nor Prophets. Neuertheles they may be assured, they shall be as they euer haue bene , subiecte to his plages

Englishemē will nether be Apostles Prophets nor good men.

and punifhments: and fo will he haue a
do with them, thogh they would haue
noght to do with hym. Yf the temperall
fworde had bene committed to the A-
poftels, as wel as was the fpirituall: if
they had bene Pears of a realme, and
knowen fo wel their duetie towarde
God and their contrye, as they did to
Chrift and his Churche, being Apoftels,
woulde they haue lyfted vp their fworde agaynft Goddes glorie, to the fub-
nerfion of the trueth and their nation,
at the commandement of their Prince
and kinge? Or wolde they not rather ha
ue anfwered: we are appoynted of God
to fet forthe his glorie, and to defend
his people, and cannot therfore obeye
you? If that woulde not ferue, muft they
then haue ceafed at their threatninges with death and difpleafure? Is that
fufficient to difcharge them, if in not v-
fing their power to fuppreffe tyranny and idolatrie, they fuffer the people of God to be deuoured? Iudge
you your felues that beare this Name, whither God coulde approue their
doinges.

*How
fhould they
iudge well
of other
més matte-
res, that cö
demne thé
felues in
their owne*

Mata-

Matathias that worthie Captay-
ne of the Iewes, as it is wryten in the fir 1. Mac. 2
ste boke of the Machabees, coulde not
so lightly excuse him self when he was
commanded by the cruel officiers of
wicked Antiochus (which had spoyled
their Tepel, rased their waules, murthered their brethern, and set vp idolatrie,
in so muche as all for the most parte,
applied them selues to their wicked par
suations) that he, with the residue shulde forsake the Lawes and sacrifices of
their God, to worshipp strange Goddes:
he made answere, to the officer of An- *A notable*
tiochus the kinge (which would to God *answere*
our Noble men had perfetly learned) *for all true*
That thoghe all Nations appartey- *Christians*
ning to kinge Antiochus shulde o- *to practise.*
beye him, so that euery man would
declyne from the Lawes of his countrie: yet I, (saieth he) my children, and
brethern, wil stand in the conuenant of
our fathers &c. Which thing he performed in dede to the glorie of God, to
his owne saluation, and comforte of his
brethern and countrie for euer.
And euen at the self same ty-

me he slewe, not onely a Iewe, one of his
owne brethern, which came to sacrifice
in his presence at the alter Modim, according to the prescript of Antiochus:
but killed also the kiges officer, that có
pelled him therto, and afterwarde di-
stroyed the altar, ād folowed the Lawe
of God with a zeale, as did Phinees. Matathias had then a litle power amongest
his brethern, but nothing to defende
him self agaynst the kinge, and also
being charged with children and kins-
folk (which semed to be all his power)
woulde nether pollute him self, nor suffer thē to be polluted with wicked idolatrie, nor causeles, to be oppressed with
Matathias   tyrannie. And yet we reade of no aucto-
was no   ritie or office he had to excuse him by:
publik   but onelie this one thing which was co-
persone.   mon to all other of his natió, the Lawes
of their countrie, and couenant of their
fathers. Which cause he thoght sufficiēt
to discharge his cóscience before God,
and to approue his doings. For as muche
as God had commanded him not onely
to denie to do the commandement of
the cruell tyrant Antiochus (vnder whó
all Ierusalem then was by conqueste)
but

but manfully to professe him and his, as
open aduersaries to his Lawes and to re
siste idolatrie by force, in killing the
idolatrer and the kinges seruant (by
whom he was compelled) and in subuer
ting the altar, where vpō the idolatrous
sacrifice shuld haue bene done. Which was, as you see, manifeste resisting
of the superior power, being but mā, to
the intent he might shewe true obedien
ce to his Lorde and God, in defending
and maynteyning his Lawes (which he
calleth the couenant of their fathers)
yea and with the temporal sworde to
the vttermost of his power. Thē if Matathias herein did discharge his con-
sciéce before God and man, in resisting
by temporal power the kinge, his commandements and officiers: it is not onely the office of Apostles ād preachers, to
resist, but the dewtie likewise of all o-
thers according to their estate and voca
tion. But you will say perchance, that
this boke of the Macabees is not of sufficient auctoriie to persuade your consciences in the like case, because it is
not reputed to be amongest those bo-
kes which are autentique, and named

Loke wel vpon this example al ye inhabitantes of Englande

Canonical. Trueth it is, but that thou (which art in like and better estate, because of thy power and auctoritie, wherewith thou art as wel charged before God as kinge or Emperour) mayst and shuldest with a safe conscience, folowe this worthie example, it is moste true and certayne. For the facte of Mattathias dependeth not vpon the auctoritie of the boke, wherin it is conteyned: but vpon the worde of God, whervpon it was grownded. For hathe he done anie otherwise in his vocation, then the Apostles did in theirs? Did not they say, that God is to be obeyed rather then man? And so sayed Mattathias, and muche more playner: that thoghe all nations woulde obeye Antiochus: yet he, and so many as he coulde procure, shulde obeye the true God and his Lawes. And like as the Apostles, according to their answer, openlie and playnly in sight of the people did vse the spiritual sworde, manfully fighting agaynst all rebellion of man in Goddes cause: so did Mattathias vse the temporall sworde according to his power,

moued

Mattathias fact depēdeth not of the auctoritie of the historybut of the worde of God.

Mattathias doing ãd the Apostls are both like.

moued by the fame reafon agaynft i-
dolatrie and oppreffion which is manifefte rebellion agaynft God . Yea and
if their were nether example nor Scripture to proue his facte: yet would verie
natural reafon compel euery man to
alowe the fame, as mofte Godlie . And
that therin he did nothing but his duetie , which thing was approued in the
iudgement of that age, and as a lawful facte and monument wryte and
left to be red and practifed of all pofteritie, the Lawe of nature fo directing
their iudgments.

But to put you out of all doute,
we will confirme it with an other te-
ftimonie moft furely auctorifed, and
the very fame in effect, of that re-
nowmed and worthie Capitayne Iofua, *Iofua made*
the fonne of Nun , whome God him *the like*
felf had chofen to fuccede Moyfes in *anfwere to*
the gouernement, and leading of the *the Ifrae-*
lites.
people of Ifrael : who after he had *Iofue. 24.*
declared the benefites of God do-
ne vnto them , from the tyme that
he had chofen them to be his people,
(namelie to Abraham whom he cal-

led from idolatrie , to Isaac and Iacob,
and to the rest of the people, their poste
ritie , in deliueringe them out of Egypt,
preseruinge them in the wildernesse ,
and geuing to them his Lawes) spake these wordes to the Elders ãd all the
multitude , sayng : Now therfore feare
ye the Lord, serue him vnfaynedlie and
faithfullie , take away the Goddes which your fathers worshipped , beyonde
the Riuer , and in Egypte, and serue the
Lorde. But yf you wil not serue the Lorde , chose vnto you this day whom you
will serue: whither ye wil serue the God
des beyonde the Riuer , or the Gods of
the Amorites in whose lande ye dwele.
As for me and my familie,we will serue
the Lorde : answering as did Matathias.

The papists
wil saye,
becaufe he
was olde
that he
doted.

And this spake he in his later dayes, to
admonishe them afore hande not to in-
cline to idolatrie and to neglecte the
Lawes of God , which is the cause of all
euill , and gapp to all mischiff . Which
sayng of Iosua, the true seruãt of God,
seemed so Godlie in the sight of all the
people , that all were compelled with a
uehemencie of spirite to say : God forbid , that we shulde forsake the Lorde,
                                          to

to serue strange Goddes. For the Lorde
our God him self, broght vs out of E-
gypt and from the house of bondage.

What wilt thou more to proue this
facte of Mattathias, ãd therbie thy duetie also, whither thou be of the Seniors
of the people, or of the multitude? Here
is thy confession, if thou be of God. Yf
all men would serue strange Godds, yet
will I and my familie serue the liuing
Lorde. And agayne, God forbid that we
shulde leaue the obedience of our God,
by whome we are created, redemed
and saued, to serue strange Goddes. And
how caneste thou say that thou seruest
God thy Lorde, except thou vse all suche means as he hath geuen to thee in
defence of his glorie, beit counsel, learning, auctoritie, power in bodie or in
soule? All muste serue the Lorde, when
he demaundeth it. And when demaundeth God these thinges of vs, if not then
chiefflie, whẽ Satã begynneth to rage, the
worde of God despiced, his Name blasphemed, his Churche scattered, his children miserably oppressed, imprisoned,
famished and murthered? Either now
muste the counsele of the Coũseller, the

*Forget not
this yf ye
feare God
and loue
your liues.*

f.

Other now
serue the
Lorde or
neuer.
Luk. 3.

learning of the learned, the auctoritie
of the honorable, the power of the Nobles, the bodies of the subiectes serue
the Lorde, or neuer. For now will the Lor
de trye who are his people in separating
the chaffe fró the corne, those that loue
the Lorde vnfaynedlie, ád wil serue him
in dede from the halting dissemblers ád
hypocrites, who thínking therby to esca
pe present daúgers, runne headlonge to
their owne destructió, thínking therby to
escape the fearefull voyce of the Lorde,
fall in to the pit. And if they came foor-
the of the pit, they are taken in the net,
and cannot escape saithe the Lorde.

Esá. 24.
Iere. 48
Hosea. 6

    There is no waye but one, to turne
agayne vnto the Lorde, who hathe woú
ded vs, and he will heale vs : he hathe
striken vs, for our synnes, and he will
bynde vs vp agayn, ád within two dayes will herestore vs to lyffe, ád the thirde day rayse vs vp, and we shal come
before his face saithe the Prophet. And
by what other means can we turne vnto
the Lorde to be healed of our woundes,
to be restored to lyffe agayne, to be lif-
ted vp and broght before his presence:
but

Repent o
countrie-
men your
vnlawfull
obedience,
ád now at
last turne
to your
Lord God

but by vnfayned repentance, euerie man of what estate, or condition so euer he be? Considering with teares how shamefullie he hathe fallen from God, and by what means, and to call for grace and strength to turne back by the self same means and wayes, to obey God in walking the contrarie. And to folowe the counsell of the Apostle, that as before we haue geuen our members to serue vnclennes and iniquitie: so now (after true repentance) make them to serue rightousnes and holynesse. Wher before we serued men and not God, now to serue God and not man, but in God: Where as we abused all the gyftes of God to mayntayne idolatrie and tyranny, now to vse the same to the restoring of Gods glorie, and preseruation of his humble and afflicted children: where as before we haue troughe contempt of his graces, especiallie the worde and Gospel of our Sauiour Iesus Christe broght vpon vs shame and confusion, now by reuerent receauing of them agayne, and framing our liues thervnto, we may remoue these plagues, ād finde

Rom. 6.

God grant this for Christes sake, to sinke in your myndes.

fauore ād grace in the sight of our God, who for this cause hathe striken vs, and by all maner of means callethe vs backe from our wickednesse, readier to receaue vs, then we to desier him.

CHAP. VIII.

The conclusion of these two parts with a farther declaration of the same, that it is both Lawful and necessarie some tymes to disobeye and also to resiste Vngodly magistrats and wherin.

Vherfore (deare brethern in the Lorde)to returne to our pourpose, you may well vnderstāde of these thīgs which haue bene hitherto mentioned, not only the cause of all our miserie in England this day, to haue bene for that we nether taught, knewe, nor vsed true obedience: but also what obediēce God requireth of all mē, ād what he cōdemnethe for disobedience. Obedience is to heare God rather then man, and to resiste man rather then God, as by the answere and doinges of the Apostles, and examples of others ye haue bene instructed. Whereī you may see how lit

Obedience

le

le the commandments, threatnynges,
power, auctoritie, or punishments of a-
nie kinge, Prince or Emperour, oght
to preuayle with vs agaynst the commandement of God, where with we a-
re charged.

Can we then pretende ignoraunce *Ignorance*
any more? Beholde, verie nature doth *can not*
teache all men, which be not destitute *excuse you*
of their comō sense ād reason, that God *much lesse*
oght rather to be obeyed then man: in *when the*
trueth is so
so muche as the Apostles therin feared *plainlye*
not the iudgment of their enimies. *taught.*

Shall auctoritie of man, or power of
Princes bleare our eyes anie lóger: seing *We must*
there is none so ignorant whose consi-*not yelde*
ciéce doth not beare him witnesse, that *to autori-*
God is moste worthie of all honor, and *tie and*
onely to be feared for his power: who *power.*
made the heauens and the earthe, and
man ruler therof, by whose power and
wisdome, as all thinges were created,
so by his wonderful prouidence are all
thinges preserued and gouerned?

Shall the threatnings of man or *Threanin-*
punishment of Princes moue vs to leaue *ges oght*
vndone that which he commandeth, ād *not to feare*
our vocation requireth? Shulde we ho- *vs.*

f. iiij

nour thē for their offices and great titles, becaufe they are called kīges, Princes, or Emperours? This mufte we do fo longe as they will be fubiectes to God, and promoters of his glorie, of whome they haue their auctoritie, as the examples of the Godlie Patriarkes, and Prophets, of Chrifte him felf, and his Apoftles, and of all martyrs in all ages vntil this day. Which with their bloude haue fealed vp this doctrine for an vndouted veritie: that there is no obedience agaynft God, which in his iudgment is not manifefte rebellion.

This doctrine of obediēce, is dayly fealed with the bloude of Sainctes

Doeft thou then vnfaynedly beleue in God, and hafte geuen thy felf to ferue him, and after art commanded of thy Prince or Ruler, what name fo euer he beare, to committ idolatrie in worfhippīg a piece of bread for thy Sauiour (as do the Papiftes) which is open blafphemie agaynft the Sonne of God?

Arte thou willed to be prefent at the idole feruice, which the Apoftle S. Paul forbiddeth: or ells to make, or erect images in Churches or tēples, to heare Maffes, to trot on pilgremage, to purcheffe pardōs, to cōfeffe the Popes auctoritie, to efteme Gods worde for herefie?

Art thou charged to be a tormentour of the Sainⱡts of God, to lay holde vpõ thē as did the Scribes ād Pharisies, the chief Bishopp and Priests whith their officiers vpon Christe and his Apostles: to bringe them before the Concile to caste then in prison, to flatter them to reuile thē opēly, to famishe them secreatly, and hange them in their gayles, to racke them, to bringe them to the galows, to the stake, and cõsumyng fier: to see execution done vpon then, as vpon theues, murtherers, villains, whoremongers, adulterours, traytors, idolaters, & blasphemers: when inwardlye thy conscience cryeth vnto thee, Take heede ād beware what thou doest to thesemen, for they are the verie seruantes of God, as Pilate was admonished by his wiffe? Art thou (I saye) cõmanded to do anie of these thiges, and fearest God? Beholde, here art thou taught what answere it behoueth thee to make, and that by the Apostles of Christe: which is, Iudge you whither it be lawfull in Godds sight to obey you rather then God. And agayne, God must be obeyed before man.

The Shirefs lealers and other inferior officers condemned

Mat. 27. Euery mãs answere to vnlaufull disobedience.

f. iiii.

Loſſe of liuinges is not a ſufficiēt excuſe to indāger thy ſoule.

If thou wilt alleadge the daunger of loſinge thy lyuing and office, wherby thou and thy familie are founde : conſider it is a greater matter to loſe thy ſoule, and to bring the curſſe of God vpon thy whole houſholde, to whome it were farre better to begg in the feare of God, thē to be gyltie of innocēt bloud,

God is the reuenger of inocentes bloude.
Pſal. 9.

which the Lorde muſt nedes reuēge according to his promeſſe. Yf thy innocēt brother, which is broght to thee, becauſe he is the ſeruant of God, be ready for Chriſtes ſake to offre vp his life in ſacrifice : what great thing is it for thee to offre vp thy vile liuing for the

Mat. 16.

ſame cauſe of rightouſneſſe? For as he in loſinge his life hath aſſurance to finde it euerlaſtingly : euen ſo mayſt thou be aſſured in forgoing thy office, becauſe thou wilt be no tormentour of Goddes children, agaynſt thy duetie

To looſe in the world, is to gayne in the heauens.
Mat. 10.
Pſal 105,

and conſcience, to haue the rewarde of rightouſneſſe at the hands of God, who eſtemeth all thinges done to anie of theſe litle ones, as done to him ſelf: and forbideth thee to touche them, ſayng, Touche not myne anoynted ones.

Ther-

Therfore, as there is no power or punishment that shuld cause thee to do euil: so is there no office or promotion, which thou shuldest not willingly forgoe, rather then in reteyninge it to be an instrument of iniurious oppression, hauing this rule of our Sauiour Christe alwayes before thine eyes: What so euer ye would that men shulde do to you, that do you to them also. *Mat.7.*

Neither is this ynough, rather to suffer iniurie and losse, then that thou wouldest be a worker of iniurie to others by any means: but more ouer it is thy parte to be a withstander of euil, and a supporter of the Godly to the vttermoste of thy power, as thou hast partly harde all ready, ãd partly shalt heare now folowing. For as God hath not created vs for our selues, but to seke his honor and glorie, and the profit of our neighbour, especially of such as be of the housholde of faithe: euen so are we idetted to God, to bestowe all those gyftes, be they spiritual or corporal, wherewith God hath blessed vs to the self same end, stryuing agaynst all impediments, helping, defending, comforting, *withstand the euil, ãd supporte the Godly*

Gen. 2.
1.Cor.10.
Gala.6.

Our detts to God.

Defend, helpe, conforte, and deliuer the godly oppreſſed, and deleuer your owne ſoules.
Exod 23.

and deliuering to the vttermoſte of our power all ſuch as we are aſſured do feare God, and ſtande in nede of our ayde and ſupporte. Otherwiſe we ſhewe our ſelues to haue more compaſsion vpon brute beaſtes, as our neighbours oxe, aſſe, or ſhepe, which Gods Lawe dothe charge vs to helpe, ſaue, or drawe forthe of the diche, althoghe it were the beaſte of our enemie.

Shall we helpe our neighbours beaſt and not him ſelfe?

Are we then bound to do this to vnreaſonable and brute beaſtes, yea to any thing belonging to our neighbour, and ſhall we be afrayde to do the like to him ſelf, what tyme he is in neceſsitie? Yf his ſhepe or other of his cattel were readie to be deuoured in our preſence of wolues, or ſuche wilde beaſtes: are we not bounde as wel in conſcience as by the Lawe of God, to driue the wilde beaſte awaye and ſaue his cattel, who can deny this to be our duetie? Can we be excuſed then in ſuffringe the ſoules and bodies of the children of God our brethern, to be moſte pitifully diſtroyed of Gods enemies, by falſe doctrine and cruel murthering, and put not to our handes and power to deliuer them?

them?

The verie Gentils with out God were taught so muche of nature, that to do wronge to a nother is not onely iniurie, but also they condemne him as an iniurious persone, which can , and will not withstande wróge done to a no ther. Wo be to thee thé(ô miserable Englande)amonge other nations and peoples, which hast a longe tyme delited in iniustice and cruel oppression. Wo be vnto you moste vngodlye and careles counsellers . Wo be to you Rulers and Magistrats, from the hieste to the loweste: for that you ruling with out the feare of God, see your owne fleshe ãd bloude , the very lãbes of God dayly to fall by flockes , not in to the diche or pit, but in to the vnsaciable mouthes of the woluefhe papistes: not onely to be hurte and iniuried , but cruelly to be deuoured both bodie and goodes , and their poore wiues, children, and families destroyed, ãd go a begginge . And yet neither the sorouful sobbes, ãd cótinual tea res of the lamétable mothers, nor the piti ful crye of the spoyled infátes, nor the ex treame necessitie of their dispersed ser

Not to withstande euill, the very Gentils cödéned as iniurie.

wo to England and her vngodly Magistrates.

The woluefhe papists .

your horrible plagues are at hãde yf ye améd not.

Ye haue
your hono-
urs to d fē
de and hel
pe the go
dly, yea ād
all others
from oppreſ
ſion and in
iurie.

Eſai. I.

The Genti
les ſhall
condemne
you in the
workes of
the lawe.
Rom. 2.

uāts, beſides the ſhamefull betrayinge
ād ſubuertiō of the whole Realme daylie approchinge, can once moue your
harde ād ſtonie hartes with pitie to defende their cauſe, and delyuer them frō
tyranny : beinge promoted to your ho-
nours and offices to that end. Can you,
eſcape the condemnation of the Lawe,
whiche prefer the preſeruation of your
beaſtes and cattell to the pretious lyues
of your owne brethern, the Image of
the liuinge Lorde, whom you are bounde to loue as your ſelues ? Shall not
the Gentils, whiche lyue beſides the Lawe, ſtand in iudgment agaynſte you
whiche profeſſe the Lawe, when they
are more preſte to defende their people from iniuries, then you yours?
Your owne offices, auctoritie, and power, ſhall in that daye put you to ſilen-
ce, and confounde you.

    Was there euer the like contempt
of Gods worde in Capernaum? The like
idolatrie amonge the heathen? Or like
tyranny and cruell murthering at Ieruſalem ? And yet to Capernaum Chriſt
hathe threatned that it ſhall be eaſier
for Tyre and Sidon in the laſt day, then
for

Luk. 10.

for it. The Gentiles he commanded to be diſtroyed as his extreame enimies. And as for Ieruſalem that worthie Citie of the Lorde, eſcaped not his ſeuere iudgement: not leauinge one ſtone vpon a nother, as oure Sauiour him ſelf afore prophecied, ãd as their miſerable ſtate and diſpertion this daye doth teſtifie. Will God then ſpare Englande alone, and puniſhe all other nations for leſſe impietie?

Nomb.33.
Exod.23.
and.34.

Mat.24.

Englande ſhall not eſcape.

Can he of his iuſtice ſpare you counſellers, you Nobles and inferior officers: Whiche ſpare not to ſpoyle, oppreſſe, accuſe, condemne, and murther the people of God, to deface his glory, and to diſtroye the whole Engliſhe Natiõ from the earthe, ſo moche as in you lieth?

Repent, repent you miſerable mẽ: for your ſynnes be at the higheſt, your cupp of iniquitie is full, and the houre of your heuy viſitation is come: when it will be to late for you to flee from the great wrath of Gods indignation, whiche ſhortlye is like to be powred vpon you. Then ſhall you well perceaue that there is no ſaluation but vnder

Repent ſhortly: for Goddes heauy wrath is at hande Eſai.29.

Gods protection, no comforte with out
Christe, no obedience agaynst God, no
power that can difpence with the charge of the Almightie and his commandements: efpeciallie when all your counfels agaynft him and his poore feruants fhall fall vpon your owne heades: your wifedome turned to follie,
your nobleneffe to vileneffe, your rule
and dominion taken from you, and you
made flaues to others: your fayre howfes and gorgeous buildinges deftroyed,
your great poffeffions geuen to your e-
nimies, your wiues to be rauifhed, your
mayds deflowred, and children murthered with out mercy, your pride and hie
lokes abated, your welthe turned to mi
ferie, your delicate faare and coftlie a-
parell to extreame hunger and begge-
rye, your ioye and paftance to weepin-
ge and continuall forrowe, and in the
end fhamefull deathe as you haue deferued. And why? Bycaufe you haue cho
fen to obeye man rather then God, and
fought rather to mayntayne your owne
pride and dignitie, then his honor and
glory.

*The caufe
of all thefe
miferies.*

*Write this
vpon your
dore poftes
ád in your
weldeck-
ed chábers.
For it will
fuerly come
yf ye repèt
not.*

And

And therfore beholde ô prowde man, *Iere. 50.*
I am come to thee (saithe the Lorde of
hostes) becaule thy daye is come, and
the tyme when i will visite thee. For the
prowde shall fall and be diftroyed, and
there shall be noman to lift him vp. I
will kindle a fire in his Cities, that shall
consume all thinges aboute them,
&c.

And iustly maye the Lorde do all this
to you, seinge he gaue you not this dignitie, makinge you Coûsellers, Noble
men, Rulers, Iustices, Mayers, Shireffs,
Bayliffs, Counstables, or Gaylers to ex-
alt your selues agaynst his Maiestie, *The end of*
and to fight agaynst Christe and his *all offices*
members: but to humble your selues in
his presence, to promote his glorie, and
to defende all those whom he committed to your charge. How commeth it
then to passe, that ye haue thus betrayde him and his people, in banishinge his
truthe to receaue falsehod, and haue
changed Religion in to superstition,
true honoringe of God, in to blasphemous idolatrie, and now (to fini-
she your procedinges) are readye to

The Spa-
niardes are
godles

to fell your fubiects for flaues to the
prowde Spaniards, a people with out
God.

That wicked woman, whom you
vntruely make your Quene, hath (faye
ye) fo cõmanded. O vayne & miferable
men. To what vileneffe are you broght,
and yet as men blynd, fee not? Becaufe
you would not haue God to raigne o-
uer you, and his worde to be a light vnto your footeftepps, beholde, he hath
not geuen an hypocrite onely to raigne
ouer you(as he promifed)but an Idola-
treffe alfo : not a man accordinge to his
appoyntment, but a woman, whiche his
Lawe forbiddeth, and nature abhorreth : whofe reigne was neuer counted
lawfull by the worde of God, but an
expreffe figne of Gods wrathe, and notable plague for the fynnes of the people. As was the raygne of cruell Iefabel, and vngodlie Athalia, efpeciall in-
ftrumentes of Satan, and whipps to his
people of Ifrael.

This you fee not, blynded with i-
gnorance : yea, whiche is more fhame,
where as the worde of God freethe you
from the obedience of anie Prince, be

Maries
vnlauful
gouerne-
ment.

Iob.34.

God forbid
deth wo-
men to rai-
gne, and
nature ab-
horreth the
fame.

he

he neuer so mightie, wise, or politike, commanding anye thinge whiche God forbiddeth, and herein geueth you auctoritie to withstand the same, as you haue harde: Yet are you willingly become as it were, bondemen to the lustes of a most impotent and vnbrydled woman: a woman begotten in adultrie a bastard by birthe, contrarie to the worde of God ād your owne lawes. And therfore códemned as a bastarde by the iudgement of all Vniuersities in Englāde, France, and Italie: as well of the Ciuilians, as Diuines. For now are we freede from that Iewesshe yoke to rayse vp seede to our brethern departing with out issue, by the comyng of our Sauiour Iesus Christe, who hathe destroyed the walle and distāce betwixt the Iewes and Gentiles, and hathe no more respecte to anie Tribes (for conseruation wherof this was permitted) but all are made one in him with out distinction, which acknowledge him vnfaynedlie to be the Sonne of God and Sauiour of the worlde. For in Christe Iesus there is nether Iewe nor Gentile, Grecian or Barbarous, bonde nor free, &c. And therfore

Marie a bastard.

Reade Halles **Cr**onicle in the 24.of the reinge of kinge Henry.8. Oxfarde. Cambrige. Orliance. Paris. Angiers. Burges. Bononie. Padua. Tholosa. Leu.10 Deu.19 Eph.2. Gala.3.

g.

it muſte nedes followe, that kinge Henrie the eight, in marying with his brothers wife, did vtterly contemne the free grace of our Sauiour Ieſus Chriſte, which longe before had deliuered vs from the ſeruitude of that lawe: and also committed adulterous inceſt contrary to the worde of God, when he begate this vngodlie ſerpent Marie, the chief inſtrument of all this preſent miſerie in Englande.

kinge Henry cõmitted inceſt in begettinge Marie.

And if any would ſaie, it was of a zele to fulfyll the lawe which then was abrogated, he muſt confeſſe alſo that the kinge did not marie of carnall luſte, but to rayſe vp ſeede to his brother: when the contrarie is well knowne to all men. Let no man therfore be offended, that I call her by her propre name, a baſtarde, and vnlawfully begotton: ſeing the worde of God, which cãnot lye, dothe geue wittneſſe vpon my parte. And moreouer, that ſuche as are baſtardes ſhulde be depriued of all honor: in ſo muche as by the Lawe of Moyſes they were prohibited to haue entrance in to the Cõgregatiõ or aſſembly of the Lorde to the tenth generation. Conſider thē your vngodlie proceadinges in defraw-

Deu.23.

ding your cõtrie of a lawfull kinge: and
preferringe a baſtarde to the lawful begotten dawghter, and exaltinge her
whiche is, and will be a comon plague ãd
euerſion of altogether: for as muche as
ſhe is a traytor to God, & promisbreaker
to her deareſt frindes, who helpinge her
to their power to her vnlawfull reigne, were promiſed to inioye that religion which was preached vnder kinge
Edwarde: which not withſtanding in a
ſhorte ſpace after, ſhe moſte falſely o-
uerthrewe and aboliſhed. So that now
both by Gods Lawes and mãs, ſhe oght
to be puniſhed with death, as an opẽ ido
latres in the ſight of God, ãd a cruel mur
therer of his Saits before mé, ãd merciles
traytoreſſe to her owne natiue coũtrie.

*The Goſ-
pellers ho
lpe her to
the crown
and ſhe ba
niſheth thẽ.*

For Gods worde ſhe abhorreth, Antichriſte hathe ſhe reſtored, her fathers La
wes contemned, her promeſſe brokẽ, and
her brother Godly kinge Edwarde as an
heretique condemned: not thinkinge it
ynoughe to expreſſe her tyranny vpon
the that liued, except ſhe ſhewed cruel-
tie, or rather a raging madneſſe on the
bodies of Gods ſeruãts lõge before buried, drawíg thẽ forth of their graues to

*M. Bucer
Paulus
Phagius,
maiſtris
Martyr,
&c.*

g. ii.

burne thē as heretikes. And in fine vtterly abhorring the Englishe nation, hath
ioyned her self to adulterous Philip, the
Spanishe kinge: to whome she hathe,
and dothe continually labor to betray
the whole kingdome. And yet ye cannot, or will not see it, nether yet for all
this be stirred vp to bridell her affecti-
ons, and withstand her vngodly doinges, to promote the glorie of God, and
to preserue your brethren, and your selues : but thinking to reteyne your pro-
motions by flattery, do hastelie drawe
Gods vengeance vpon your selues and
others.

who is more blind then they that can and will not see? Here vnto the lawes of the real me, the will and prophe cie of her father doth prouok thē

For do you thinke that Philip will be
crowned kinge of Englande, and reteyne in honor Englishe counsellers ? Will
he credite them withe the gouernement
of his estate, who haue betrayed their
owne? Shall his nobilitie be Spaniardes,
with out your landes and possessions?
And shall they possesse your promotiōs
and lyuinges, and your heads vpō your
shulders ? Come they to make a spoyle
of the whole Realme, and leaue you ād
yours vntouched? Where is your great
wisdome become? Your subtile counsels
and

and policies, where of you bragge so
muche, to whome these thinges be hid,
that euerie childe espieth?

If Esai the Prophet had not forespo
ken these secret iudgments of God, in
blynding the eyes of the prowde con-
temners, I coulde not cease to wonder
at your grosse ignorance, as now I consi
der with greife of harte, the miserie
which is like shortly to come vpon you
in full measure, for this calamitie, alreadie powred vpon others, through your
procurements and studies. Which fearefull iudgment of God loke neuer to
escape, except suddaynlie ye repent and
change your vngodlie purpose. If you
be at a couenant with deathe (as you
thinke) you shall not auoyde it, if you
thinke to escape the comon destructiõ,
making dissimulation and lyes your
refuge, yet shall you be reuealed: for
the Lord him self will destroye all your
counsels, because they are not of him.

Yt is not your going to the Masse,
your praysing of the Pope, your flat-
tring of your Quene, and shauen Priests of Baal, that can defende you in

Esa.3.
4 29.

Esai. 28.

that day:nether yet your licences whiche some of you purchaffe of an infidel
to departe out of your countrie , fome
lyinge in idolatrous places,differing no
thinge from them in ther diffolute liui
nge,fome paffinge in to Italie to pleafe
their Quene, and to get an opinion of
men that theyapproue her procedings,
rather coueting to haue the name of a
blafphemoufe papifte , then of Chrifte
our Sauiour.Thikinge by fuche vnlawfull meanes to worke miracles:but their
gunes at length will be confufion ,as
now their frute whiche they haue
brohgt thence do witneffe : that is the
want of Gods feare and open diffimu-
lation.

This is not the way (ô vaine men) to
winne Gods fauour, and to efcape his
fearfull iudgmentes : but to increafe
his wrathe and hafté his vengeance,who
will not be mocked, nether fuffer his
holye Name lôge to be blafphemed.Cô
fider with your felues , and returne to
the right way , and walke in it while ye
haue tyme, and I will fhewe it vnto
you.

YOV

Licences pur-hafed of infidels and lyinge in idola-trous pla-ces is tho ught good inough of carnall gof pelers.

Their de aus proue what they be.

You haue synned moste greuouslie agaynst the Lorde: knowe your transgressions, and with teares confesse thé, euery man vnfaynedlie vnto the Lorde, who is redie to mercie and slowe to anger. You haue despised and abused the worde of his dearely beloued Sonne Iesus Christ, the Author of saluatió, in the dayes of our Godlie kinge Edwarde (which is the cause why God hath thus plaged vs with a tyrant) seke after the worde agayne and receaue it with all reuerence. By geuing auctoritie to an idolatres woman ye haue banished Christe and his Gospell, and in his place restored Antichriste with all his infections, wherin your owne consciences condemne you of euil. Then in takinge agayne the same auctoritie from her, you shall restore Christe and his worde and do well. In obeyinge her, ye haue disobeyed God. Then in disobeying her, ye shall please God. Because you haue geuen place to her and her counsells, you are all become idolatrous hypocryts, and also traytors to your owne Countrie: then by resisting her

The onely means to escape miserie. Psal. 103.

Folowe wyse counsel, least ye and al your land perishe.

felues damnation for their tranfgreffió
and her wicked decrees, you muft be
made true worfhippers of God, ád faithfull Englifhe men.

Other meás there are not, but to turne to God by repentáce, to banifhe fal-
fehode by receauíg the trueth, to ouerthrowe Antichrifte , and all kinde of i-
dolatry by honoring Chrifte and his
Gofpell : to fuppreffe tyranny by iufti-
ce : to withftande oppreffion and murther by defending the iufte and innocent, and punifhing the workers of ini-
qùitie, of what eftate or condicion fo e-
uer they be , as after(God willing)fhall
be proued at large.For as by this means

Reftore
goddes ho
nour and ef
cap: Gods
vengeance

onely Gods honor muft be reftored,and
you efcape his vengeance,to obeye thé
that obeye God , and refifte them that
refifte his Maieftie,rédringe vnto all accordinge to his Lawes: euenfo , when
they fhulde vnderftand that their fubiectes be no more as it were brute beaftes with out fenfe or iudgment:but that
they knowe wherein, ád how farre they
owe obediéce,ád would no more be led
by their deuilifhe and vngodlie luftes,
as they haue bene and yet are pre-
fentlie ,

Then woulde their Princes and
Rulers alſo geue them ſelues with all
diligence, to ſtudie and applie the ſame
Lawe of God : then woulde they do nothinge them ſelues, nor commande o-
thers, where in they where not aſſured
to pleaſe him. Then woulde they learne to obeye God, which now rebel a-
gaynſt him : and to folow the examples
of the Godlie kings and Rulers, hauing
the boke of the Lorde euer with them,
neuer ſuffring it to departe from them.
But as worthie Ioſua, Ioſias, and Ioſa-
phat, to reade and ſtudie in it day and
night. Not to declyne from it them ſelues, nor yet to ſuffer their ſubiects therin to be ignorãt, which is the onlie wiſedome of God and comforte of all
mens conſciences. Then ſhulde the Rulers loue and preſerue their ſubiectes.
And the ſubiects likewiſe reuerentlie
obeye their ſuperiours. To conclude,
then ſhuld all be bleſſed of God, feared
of their enimies, ſure from all daũgers,
voyde of all idolatrie and falſe religiõ,
and eſtemed of all nations the wyſeſt
and mightieſte people vpon the earthe,
as God promiſſed to Iſrael, ſo longe as

yf they knewe rightly how to obey and wherin, thẽ ſhulde theſe thinges here mentioned come to paſſe.
Deu.17.

Gods boke teache the true obediẽce.

Deu.4.

they ſhulde lyue.

CHAP. IX.

Anſwers to the contrarie obiections of ſuch as teache all maner of obedience to Magiſtrats to be lawful, taken forthe of the New Teſtament.

Vt for as muche as there is nothing ſo manifeſt and true, which is not either obſcured vtterlie by contrary reaſons of mans brayne, or ells diſcredited by other places of Scripture wrógfully vnderſtáde and applyed by many: I haue here thoght expedient before I proceade anie further, for the better eſtabliſhing of the trueth, to anſwer and ſatiſfie, ſo far as ſhal pleaſe God to geue vnto me, all ſuche reaſons, auctorities, and Scriptures, as are aleadged to the contrarie: to the intent that we may not onlye ſee the trueth, and ſo be ſtyrred to imbrace it, but alſo may eſpie the falſehod, ád learne to auoyde it.

And becauſe amongeſt all other auctorities ád reaſós, there is none of greater force thé that which is wryten in the Epiſtle of S. Paul to the Romains: we will firſte of all others begin with it. Let euerie ſoule (ſaith he) ſubmitt him ſelf

Rom. 13.

The firſte Obiection.

to the auctoritie of the higher powers:
for there is no power but of God, and
the powers that be, are ordeyned of
God. who soeuer therfore resisteth
power, resisteth the ordinance of God:
and they that resist, shal receaue vnto
them selues damnation. Here (say they)
is a general doctrine affirmed by the A-
postle, that euery man (none excepted)
must be subiecte to superiour powers:
and if euery man muste be subiect, none
oght to disobey.

Besides this, beholde the Apostle
doth not barely affirme this proposi-
tió, sayíg: Euery person (for that he mea
nethe by euery soule) must be subiecte
to the Magistrates and Rulers, of what
condition so euer he be, but proueth
the same with a moste sure argument ga
thered of the ordinance of God: because
there is no power but of God. And therfore to resiste powers, is to resiste God
him self, whose ordinance it is. And not
contented with one reason, he confirmeth the same with a nother depen-
ding of Gods punishments, which he
hath appoynted for all them that resiste, which is, to receaue to them
selues damnation for their transgressió;

so that they cōclude, that it is not onely
Paules auctoritie that maketh all men
subiecte to their superiours (which notwithstanding were sufficient, being the
Apostle of Christe) but also the same is
by good and stronge reasons confirmed.

Answere

In answering to this obiection, I will
not longe holde you in rēdring the cause, which as we may probably gether
The cause mould the Apostle to write this to the
wherfore Romains cōcerning obedience to their
the Apostle superiours: but in few wordes touche so
was mo- muche as seemeth necessarie. It may a-
ued thus peare very credible (which some God-
to write. lie and learned do wryte) that amōgest
the Romayns, after they had receaued
the Gospel, there were many vnder that
name, which woulde be deliuered from
all subiection: thinking the office of
Magistrates nomore necessarie to them
that professed Christe: as do this day
Anabap- the Anabaptists and Libertins. Others,
tists. who had bene once freed from tribute
Libertins and custome paying, to strange Magistrates, woulde therat take an occasion
by preaching of the Gospell to paye no
more tribute to their superiours. Such
di-

were diuers of the Iewes, who couted it Denyars of
for abôdage. And that kide of secte was tribute
raysed vp euen in Christes dayes, as appeareth whê the Pharisies sent their dis-
ciples with Herodes seruátes to knowe
his iudgment, whither it were lawful for
them to paye tribute to Cæsar or no. Mat.22
And in the Actes, Gamaliel maketh
mention of one Iudas Galilæus, which Act.5.
was autor of that secte, and moued muche trouble amógest the people, sayng:
It was not lawful to paye tribute. By
these and suche like opinions, the A-
postle (perceauing the office of Magistrates to come in to contempte, and
men to esteme it not lawful, which God
him self ordeyned in defence of his religion and Ciuile policie (was moued
to wryte as is before mencioned: exhor-
ting all men to esteme the office of Magistrates as Gods ordinance, and to o-
beye them whom God had appoynted
Rulers ouer them.

Then as the Apostle wryteth we confesse, and so muche as he speaketh we
graúte, that is, that all men are bownd
to obey such Magistrates, whome God
hathe ordeyned ouer vs lawfully ac-

cording to his worde, which rule in his
feare according to their office, as God
hathe appoynted. For thogh the Apoſtle ſaith : There is no power but of God:
yet doth he not here meane anie other
powers, but ſuch as are orderly and lawfullie inſtitute of God. Ether els ſhulde
he approue all tyranny and oppreſsion,
which cometh to anie common welth
by means of wicked and vngodlie Rulers, which are to be called rightlie di-
ſorders, and ſubuerſions in comon welthes, and not Gods ordinaunce. For he
neuer ordeyned anie lawes to approue,
but to reproue and puniſhe tyrantes, i-
dolaters, papiſtes and oppreſſors. Then
when they are ſuche, they are not Gods
ordinaunce. And in diſobeying and re-
ſiſting ſuch, we do not reſiſte Gods or-
dinauce, but Satã, and our ſynne, which
is the cauſe of ſuch. Or els, if we ſhall
ſo conclude with the wordes of the A-
poſtle, that all powers what ſo euer
they be muſt be obeyed and not reſiſted, then muſt we confeſſe alſo, that
Satan and all his infernall powers are
to be obeyed. Why? becauſe they are
powers,

We may reſiſte ty rantes and yet not Godes ordinance.

By the papiſtes gatherig, Satan oght not to be reſiſted.

powers and haue their powers also of
God, which cannot touche man any
farther then God permitteth. But S. Iames geueth vs, contrarie commandement, saing: Resiste the deuel and he
will flee awaye from you.

Iob 12.
Iam. 4

And that the Apostle Paule dothe
so restrayne his wordes to all lawfull
powers, we nede not to seke far of.
For in the self same Chap. after he dothe expounde his mynde : that is, what
powers and Magistrates he meaneth :
Such(saith he)as if thou doest well, thou
nedeste not to feare, but if thou doest e-
uel. And agayne wilt thou be out of feare of the power? Do wel then : and so
shalt thou be praysed of the same. For
he is the minister of God for thy welthe.
But if thou doest euill, feare: for he bea-
reth not the sworde for noght : for he is
the minister of God, to take vengeance
of them that do euill &c. Whereby we
may playnly vnderstäde, that althoghe,
he saithe, There is no power but of God:
yet he meaneth suche power as is his or-
dinäce and lawfull: whose office städeth
in these two poyntes, to deféd the good,
and to punishe the euel: not to be feared

The proffe
of this ans-
were.

for wel doing, but for euil, to whom the
fworde is geuen for that purpofe. And
to fuch, with the Apoftle we graūt alfo,
that euery perfone muft be fubiecte ād

The papifts
argument
is fully
anfwered obedient: for they are Gods ordinaunce. And to difobey or refifte fuch, is to
difobey and refifte God him felf. And
therfore do deferue iuftlie to receaue
Gods punifhment, which, as the Apoftle
threatneth, is damnation. And this makethe nothing agaynft our former fentence, but rather confirmeth the fame:
approuīg no obedience but that which is lawful, that is to fay, according to
Gods appoyntment and ordinance, as
doth more euidētly appere in his wordes folowing: partly in that he demaundeth obedience to fuch for confcience
fake, and not for feare of vengeance o-
nely. As thogh he would faye: fo farre is
it from reafon and Gods worde that a-
ny man fhulde difobey or contemne
the Magiftrates, ordeyned by God to
punifhe vice and mantayne vertue, that
he nedeth no other to reproue him of
euil in fo doing, then his owne propre
cōfcienceé, which will (iuftly examined)
teache him how Gods ordinance oght
                              to be

to be reuerenced , especially seruing to
the preseruation of the people , in suppressing wickednesse , and promoting
Godlynesse.

For that cause he willeth after to paye
their tribute, not to euery man that will
demande (for vnlawful demandes may
be lawfully denied) but to whome tribute belongeth, custome to whom custo
me , feare to whom feare , and honour
to whom honour is due.

Obedience then he requireth of all *Obedience*
mé, tribute also, custome, feare, and ho *is commaun*
nor: but vnder this condition of iustice *ded to all*
and æquitie , to render these dueties to *men: but*
them that haue iuste title thereúto. And *yet vnder*
who are they , but (as I sayed before) *cōditton.*
such as God hath appoynted to rule o-
uer vs in his feare, for our profit, and preseruation of the comon welthe?

To this also dothe the sayng of S. Pe- *The second-*
ter wel agree, thoghe it be broght in of *de obiectiō*
the other partie to proue the contrary: *ā̄l answere*
Submit your selues to euery ordinaúce *1 Pet. 2.*
of mā for the Lordes sake: whithe: it be
to kíge as to the chief, or vnto Rulers as
vnto them that are sent of him , for the
punishment of euel doers, and the pray-

h.

se of thē that do well . Beholde how Peter here nether diſſenteth from him ſelf in his anſwere before to the Cōcile, nor here diſagreeth from Paule, willíg obedience to kinges and inferior Rulers: not to all, but to ſuch as are appoynted to puniſhe euill doers , and prayſe the contrary : and to diſobey ſuch , muſte nedes be condemned for wicked and vngodlie rebelliō . For ſuche there were as maye playnly appere by . S . Peters wordes folowing, whiche vnder the pretence of libertie woulde couer and cloke their malice . And this the Apoſtle forbiddeth in all maner of ſubiectes , and iuſtlye.

The thyrde obiection and anſwere.

But you will ſaye, the wordes of Peter folowing concerning the obedience of ſeruantes to Maiſters, dothe charge vs farther then with godlie Rulers , and ſuch as rule according to their office. For to ſeruantes he writeth on this wiſe . Seruantes obeye your Maiſters with all feare , not onely if they be good and curteous, but alſo thogh they be frowarde : for ſo the greke worde dothe ſignifie, a cōbrous, frowarde, or a perſone harde to pleaſe and ſelfe willy. Wherof they

they will conclude, that Peter commandeth obedience to all kinde of persones, good and bad: what so euer they commande must be done. and why? because he so chargeth seruants to obey their maisters.

Neuertheles this is to be obserued in reading the wordes of Peter (as also in all the holy Scriptures) that we must so take them as they agree with him self, and not agaynst him. For the Spirit of God changeth not his meaning: but what he saithe once, he saythe for euer. Saint Peter here seemeth to preuent the obiection which seruantes (desierous of libertie) might haue obiected, being willed to obey their Maisters: as thoghe he would saye: I am not ignorant that there are many Maisters troblesome, frowarde, and importune ouer you: which are not so gentle and curteous towardes you as becomethe them: well: that is their faut and infirmitie, which you must for Christes sake, whom you professe, patiently sustayne and beare. For thogh your Maisters be roughe or frowarde (he saith not wicked and vngodly) that is no

Answere.

Of what maner of maisters Peter speaketh.

h. ii.

caufe why ye fhuld not faithfully ferue
them for the tyme of your feruitude, fo
longe as they will nothing of you, but
that which is good and godlie.

Then the mynde of S. Peter is that the
fhreudneffe or frowardnes of Maifters, is
no lawful or iuft occafion why the feruantes fhulde be difobediét. And as this
is the verie meaning of the Apoftle in
that place: fo is it not like that he would
write contrarie to him felf, when he
fayed: God oght rather to be obeyed
then man. Nether can he be iudged con
trary to the Apoftle Paul, who bindeth
vp all lawful obediéce whith this knot,
In the Lorde: fpeaking vnto childré, ãd
exhortyng thé to obeye their fathers &
mothers. But how? In the Lorde faith he.
And why? For that is iuft. Then if Paule
charge not children with further obedience to their parentes, then in the
Lorde, to whom principallie they are
by Gods commandement and nature
bounde, will Peter bynde feruantes to
their Maifters anie further thé in the Lor
de? And if it be iufte obedience onlie whi
ch is in the Lorde: can ther be any lawful
obediéce agaynft him, either of childré
towardes

Act. 4.

The true
knot of
obedience.
Ephe. 6.

towardes ther parétes, feruátes towardes their Maifters, or fubiectes towardes their Rulers or Magiftrates? No, God is the firft and principal Father, Maifter ãd Lorde, to whó firfte obedience mufte be geuen as he doth demáde: and to others in him, and for him onely, as we were taught at the beginning.

God is our chief Father, Lorde and maifter.

And that S. Peter had onely refpecte to the rough condicions of Maifters, and not to their vnlawful commandement agaynft God and their confcience (which they are bownde to do for no mans pleafure) the wordes do playnelie witneffe. For this is thãkes worthye (faithe he) if a man for confcience towardes God indure grief, fuffring wongfully. For what prayfe is it, if when ye be buffeted for your faults, ye take it patientlye? &c. Then ye fee the meanyng of S. Peter is not to make vs fubiecte to anie euill or vngodlie commãdementes, but to perfuade all feruantes not to caft of their duetie, during the tyme of their feruitude, notwithftãding they be roughlie dealt. with all of their Maifters, which thing is not fpoken here of S. Peter to incourage or mayntayne

S. Peter aproueth not froward maifters.

frowarde Mafters in their frowardnes,
nor yet to forbid the feruantes which
feare God to f ke after lawful remedie
at the hãdes of fuperior powers, who for
that caufe are ordeyned tó feeiuftice ad
miniftred to all fortes of mé, as well to
feruantes as others:but th t they fhulde
not thike the fnarpneffe oftheirMaifters
to be a caufe fufficiét to f ee them from
doing their duetie vpõ the other parte.

Seruant:s oppr ffed may feke la w full remedy a gainfttheir maifters.

In like cafe may we conclude of Prin
ces ãd Magiftrats, thogh they be rough
and frowarde : yea, thoghe be fore God
they are wicked, vngodlie, and repro-
bate perfons (as was Saule)yet fo longe
as their wikedneffe brafteth not out ma-
nifeftly agaynft God, ãd his Lawes, but
outwardly will fee them obferued and
kept of others,punifhing the tranfgref-
fors,and defending the innocent: fo lon
ge are we bounde to render vnto fuch,
obedience, as to euill and roughe Mai-
fters:becaufe we may not takeGods of-
fíce in hande to iudge of the harte any
farther then their outwarde deedes do
geue manifeft teftimony. Otherwife, if
without feare they tranfgreffe Gods
Lawes them felues and cómande others
to do the like, then haue they loft that

How far wicked Princes may be obeyed.

honor and obedience which otherwise
their subiectes did owe vnto them: and
oght no more to be taken for Magistrates: but punished as priuate trãsgressors,
as after I haue promised to proue.

Here vnto they adde the saying of
our Sauiour Iesus Christe to Peter, which bad him put vp his sworde, after he
had strické the seruãt of the high Priest,
and cut of his eare: not mynding by the
sworde to make resistance. Wherevpon
they gather that althogh it be lawful in
doctrine and preaching for the seruants
of God to withstãd and reproue the enimies, as Christ him self and his Apostles
did: yet it is not permitted to do the same by anie outwarde or bodely force. For thé as Christ answered, he might
haue obtayend of his Father 12. Legions
of Angels for his defence. *The fourth obiection. Mat.26. Ioh.18.*

To this we shall sone answere, if we *Answere.*
consider who spake this, to whom, and
for what cause it was spoké. Which cir-
cumstances well waied, geue a great
light to all like facts and sayinges. First
we must diligently consider the office
of our Sauiour Iesus Christe, which
as it was in all poyntes spirituall, aswell

concerning his kingdome which he him
self affirmeth not to be of this worlde,
as his Priesthod and Prophecie : euen
so for his owne parte, coulde he vse no
temporal force or power for the accom
plesshment of the same, because he de-
nieth that he either came to raigne in
this worlde, or ells to be a iudge therin:
as he answered the man, which would
haue had him to comande his brother to
deuide the landes bewixt them, sayng:
Man, who made me a iudge or deuider
ouer you? And being demanded to geue
iudgment agaynst the woman taken in
adultrie, he woulde not take that office
vpon him, but sayd vnto the woman,
when her accusers were gone: Nether do
I condemne thee: go thy waye, and synne no more.

  Thus as concerning Christes owne
persone, who had all thinges and powers
both in heauen and in earth at his comandement, it is euident that he woulde vse no temporal power agaynst his
enimies : for that he was not therwith
charged. Which exáple taketh not waye
the office or duetie of such as are charged

Ioh 18.

Luk 12.

Ioh.8.

why Christ v-sed not the defence of the tempo-ralpower.

ged with the téporall sworde, to vse it in defence chieflye of Gods glorye, and the preseruation of those that are vnder them.

Secondly why he forbad Peter also, and in him all the reste of the Apostles, we can not be ignorant. For who knoweth not that the Apostles were witnesses of Iesus Christe chosen forthe of the worlde (as S. Iohn saithe) not to defende their Maister by the temporall sworde (for that were to vsurpe vpon a nother mans office, not apperteyninge to them) to whom onelie the spirituall sworde was comitted, to fight manfullie with it agaynst the worlde, Satan and all spirituall powers. For as the Apostle saith: Thoghe we walke compassed with the fleshe, yet do we not warre fleshlie. For the weapós of our warrfare are not carnall thinges, but stronge by the power of God to cast downe holdes: wherwith we ouerthrowe imaginatiós of euery high thinge that is exalted agaynst the knowlege of God, and bringe in to captiuitie euery thoght to the obediéce of Christe. Wherfore, seig the office of the Apostles also is spirituall,

Why Peter was forbyd to vse the sworde.

Act 1.
Ioh. 17.

Ephes 6.
Hebr 4.
2. Cor. 10.

as their Maifters was: and had onely fpirituall weapons to vfe in the defence of
the Gofpell, wherof they were minifters:

The abfur
dite of this
reafon.

it is not good reafon to conclude their
purpofe, that Magiftrates and other in
ferior officers, oght not to vfe the temporall fworde in defenfe of religion: becaufe Chrifte woulde not fuffer Peter to
fight with the temporall fworde. But rather as Chrifte requireth of Peter and
of all the reft, the faithfull vfe of the fpi
rituall fworde, where with they were
charged, or ells they fhulde be fubiecte
to malediction and iudgmét: For wo be

1.Cor.9.
As the pre
achers are
charged to
vfe the fpi-
ritual
fworde, fo
are the
Magiftrats
bonde to
fet forthe
Cods glorie
poral fw-
orde.

to me (faith Paule) if I preache not : e-
uéfo may not they efcape iudgment ád
the curfe of God, which vfe not the tem
porall fworde cómitted vnto them with
all indeuour in the defence of Cods
glorie and his Church, wherewith euery man is charged, according to his vo
cation and power, none except.

To be fhorte, if our Sauiour Chrift fhul
de, as he might by his power, haue with-
ftand the Iewes that came to apprehend
him and put him to death, how fhuld he
haue dronken of that cup which his Father had geuen him? That is, how fhul-
de

de he by his deathe and passion haue
redemed vs, for which cause he came in *Rom.5.*
to the worlde : not to haue his liffe také *Iohn. 10.*
from him agaynst his will, but willin-
glie to lay it downe for all.

Then we see that there is nothing in
this saying of Christe to Peter, which
can condemne lawfull resisting of vngodlie Rulers in their vngodly commandementes. For thogh it was profitable to all men that Christ without a-
ny resistance shulde be crucified, being
the sacrifice appoynted of God the Father to saluation : yet is it not therfore
lawfull for the inferior officers, or permitted to the subiectes, to suffre the
blasphemie and oppression of their superiors to ouerflow their whole countrie and nation, when both power and
means is geuen vnto them lawfully to
withstand it, and they by their profession and office are no lesse bounde to
put it in execution.

CHAP. X.

Obiections out of the olde Testament, and Answers
to the same.

His muche being spoké to satisfie such obiecti- ons as are comonlye al- ledged forthe of the New Testament: let vs see also what may be say ed agaynst vs in the old, and after what sorte they may be truely answered. Ie-

The firste obiection out of Ier. 29. remie they alleadge in his letter sent from Ierusalem to the captaynes in Ba- bylon, to the Priests and Prophetts, and to all the people of Israell that then we- re in Babylon, counselling them how to behaue them selues, and to escape danger. The effect wherof was this: not to rebell, that they might escape, but to remayne still and abide the ap- poynted tyme of the Lorde: yea, to se- ke the peace of the Citie wherinto God had broght them, and to praye to God for it. For (saithe he) with the peace of that Citie, shall your peace be also.

Baruch. 1. And the like is wryten in Baruch the Prophet tending to the same end, that they shulde pray for the longe liffe of Nabuchadnezer ãd Balthazer his sóne, that vnder their shaddow (that is prote- ction) they might lyue and serue them
a longe

a longe tyme. Wheerin (saye they) two
things are to be noted agaynst our o-
pinion. The firste, that he forbiddeth
them to rebell, and exhorteth them pa-
ciently to abide the tyme appoynted of
their delyuerance. The seconde, that
they are bownd to pray for their enimies, and welthe of their Cities, and
therin also are bounde to obey them.

This Epistle or letter of Ieremie sent *Answere.*
to the Iewes at Babylon then captiues,
we maye not deny to be his: thoghe of
the Prophecie of Baruch some do doute, and esteme it not as Canonicall. Neuertheles because they tend bothe to o-
ne effecte in this matter, we will admit-
te bothe. Firste, granting that their co- *The cause*
unselle to quietnes and to abstayne frõ *why Iere-*
rebellion was good and necessary: be- *mie and*
cause it proceaded from the Spirite of *Baruch*
God and of knowledge, which spake or *thus coũ-*
wrote nothing that God had not reue- *selled.*
led vnto them: and wherof they also
shuld not admonishe others, to the intẽt
they might geue no credit to false Prophetes, which woulde stirre them vp to
sedition, perswading them that they
shulde not longe continewe in Baby-

lon, when as the Lorde had other wise appoynted. Wherof when God assured them by his Prophet, it must nedes be counted extreame madnesse and rebellion agaynst God, if they shulde haue done the contrarie. As we reade of wicked Achab, who crediting the flatterig counselle of the false Prophetes, disobeyed God in conteníng the trueth tolde hī by Micheas: but to his owne destructió.

Therfore this matter is sone āswered, where we haue the secrete counselle of God reueled vnto vs, admonishing vs to abide in any place, ād not to departe til he call vs: we are more then rebells to do the contrarie, ād muste sustayne the daunger worthelye. But this is not our questió, whether we oght to remayne in any place so longe as God hathe commāded vs: but whither we oght to do euill at the commandement of Prince or power, wheresoeuer we be, or in what estate, be it neuer so miserable. For thogh Ieremie counselled thé with pacience to remayne in Babylon, yet nether he, norBaruch would permit thé to followe the exaple of the Gétills there, in idolatrie or euell doíg: as the Epistle of Ieremie

1. kinges
22.

The state
of the question.

mie set also to the Iewes captiues in Ba
bylō ād wrytten in the prophecie of Baruch, doth abundantlie witnesse. And as
the exáples of Daniel also, Sidrach, Misa
ch, ād Abdenago do teache vs: which not
wihstādīg their Captiuitie, woulde not
obey the kīges cōmandemēt to do euill.

Baruch. 6

Dani. 3.

   Also in that they are willed to pray
for the good estate of the Citie wherin
they dwelled, that is Babylō, and for the
lōge liffe of Nabuchadnezer ād his sōne
the causeis also alleadged, to the itēt that
the peace of that Citie shuld also be their peace: ād for that Nabuchadnezer ād
his sōne shuld be their shadow ād prote
ctiō, God so mouīg their hartes. Which
causes are sufficient why the people of
God shulde be thākfull, that is, to wishe
well to the places and persons where, ād
of whom they receaue any benefit, espe
cially peace and protection, as was promised to the Iewes in Babylon.

why the
Iewes we-
re willed
to pray for
Nabuchad
nezars lon
ge life.

   But what is this to the purpose? The Iewes were cōmāded of God by the Prophe
tes especiallie to tarry in Babylō, where
thē for their syns they were captiues, be
cause their owne Citie Ierusalē, ād all th
eir coútrie was destroyed ād subiecte to

Nabuchadnezer and there remayned
no other place where they might haue
peace, but in Babylon and vnder his iu-
risdiction. Is this then a sufficient excuse for you that inioye your countrie
and are charged with the defence therof, to suffer your selues willingly to be
spoyled of Gods glory, and peace of
your consciences, that is, true religion:
and you for the same cause to be oppressed, remoued and murthered, to geue place not onely to them that hate
you, but to the greatest enemies of
Christ, the papistes, and idolatrous Spaniards?

Wherfore
the Iewes
shulde be
quiet in
Babylon.

The Iewes were willed to be quiete
in Babylon, because that they and their
brethren also disperced shuld therby
finde more fauour and comforte: shall
you therfore forsake God and betraye
your countrie to bringe the vengeance of God ād his horrible plagues vpō
your selues and your brethern, wherof
you haue alreadie felt some portion?
The Iewes were willed to praye for Na
buchadnezer and his sonne, for that by
them they shulde passe ouer a great
part of their captiuitie with peace, and
be

be also by them defended from other
enemies. Are you therfore excused, that
permit your selues to be made a pray to
Satan, Antichriste, and to all sortes of
Gods enimies, at the commandement of
an vngodlie woman? Who seeketh but
to consume the Englishe nation, and in
the end to cut your throtes that nowe
are in auctoritie, whom she vseth as in-
struments, to bring her wicked purpo-
ses to passe.

Is your condition now all one with
the Iewes? In dede brethren it is like to
be muche worse, and that shortly without Gods vnspeakable mercy: but as yet
their is some difference: They were captiues ād prisoners vnder their enimies,
in a strange countrie, but you are yet in
your owne countrie and howses (thogh
moste vnnaturally you haue dryuen out
many by tyranny). You haue yet your
owne lawes amongest you, that is, the
Lawe of God ād of your Realme, if you
woulde vse them: by the which you haue had all peace ād quietnes. And in có
temning these, ye see in to what case ye
are broght, and in to what miserie, readie to fall. You may yet with Gods hel-

The mise-
rable estat
of Englãd

i,

pe, and your endeuor promote his glory, vnderprop that Realme and comon
welth,which by your falſehod is fallig
in to vtter ruine.The fall wherof,you,ād
yourſchiefly,whichhauegreateſtcharge
ſhall haue greatteſte cauſe to bewayle.

If your Ieſabell, thoghe ſhe be an vnlawfull Gouerneſſe, and oght not by
Godsword and your owne lawes to rule,would ſcke your peace and proteᶜtiō
as did Nabuchadnezer to his captiues
the Iewes: then might you haue ſome

Nabuchad
pretence to follow Ieremies counſelle:
nezer is to
that is,to be quiete, and praye for her
be preſer-
liffe,ifʃhe would cōfeſſe the onelie God
red to your
of the Chriſtians, and not compell you
Ieſabel in
to idolatrie no more then did Nabuchad
the zeale
nezer:who acknowledged theGod of the
of God.
Iewes to be the true and euerlaſting
Nabuchad
God,and gaue the ſame commādement
nezers de-
throughout all his dominiōs,Thatwhat
eree.
ſoeuer people or nation ſpake euill of
the God of Iſraell ſhuld be rent in pie-
ces,and his howſe counted deteſtable.
Ieſabel wor
For (ſaithe he) Ther is no other true
ſhippeth
God that ſo coulde deliuer his ſeruátes,
Maoxin ād
as he did Sidrach Miſach ad Abdenago.
cauſeth o-
But becauſe her doīges tēd all to the
thers to do
contrarie,that is to blaſpheme God, ād
the like.

also compell all others to do the like,
what cloke haue you here to permitte
this wickednesse?

To be shorte, if she at the burninge
of three hundreth Martyrs at the leste,
coulde haue bene satisfied ād vnfaynedly moued to confesse the true Christe
and Messias , and repented her former
rebellion in geuing contrarie commandement to all her dominions, charging
thē to receaue agayne the true religion
and to expell all blasphemous idolatrie
of the pestilent papistes: and that none
shulde speake any euill agaynst Christe
and his Religiō (as did Nabuchadnezer
by the exāple of three persōs onely, whō
the fire by the power of God coulde not
touche) then were she more to be borne
with, and reuerenced as a Ruler (if it were lawfull for a woman to rule at all)
then were there also some probabilitie
in the reasons of the aduersaries of this
doctrie. Otherwise as you nowsee, it ma
keth nothing at all for their purpose.

A nother Argumēt is gathered of the
words written in the same Prophet Iere
mie : speaking of the dominion which
God was purposed to geue vnto Nabuchadnezer kige of Babylō on this wise:

The second
obiection
out of Ie-
remie. 27.

i. ii.

I haue made the earthe ād mē(saithe the Lorde) ād the beastes vpō the earthe in my strēgth and stretched out hand, and it do I geue to him that pleaseth me. And therfore haue I geuē all this lande in to the hands of Nabuchadnezer my seruant. And all natiós and mightie kinges shall serue him, and till the tyme of his lande do come, that is, till I visite him, and his countrie also. And it shall come to passe, that I will visite the nation or kingdome which will not serue the kinge of Babell with sworde, famine, and pestiléce. Wherfore serue ye the kinge of Babell and lyue. Beholde, saye they, (who thinke it in no case lawfull to withstande vngodlie Rulers) This wicked kinge is cóstitute of God, and made his seruante. And moreouer those that shulde withstand him, are cursed and threatned with sword, famine, and pestilence. And therfore to disobey suche, muste nedes be vnlawfull.

Answere.
Ieremie.5.
wherfore
Tyrantes
are called
Gods in-
strumentes.

Nabuchadnezer as it is wrytten in Ieremie, is called the maule of the Lorde, and his instrumét of warre, by the which he was determyned to beate doune all Nations and kingdoms, punishing them

for

for their synnes and idolatrie. And therfore the Lorde calleth him his seruáte,
for that he had chosé him to that office.
Nether oght we to maruell that God
will vse the labours of vngodlye persones, seing all being his creatures are at
his commandement, as is Satan with all
his infernall spirites. Then God, hauing
appoynted Nabuchadnezer to this office to be his tormentor, as well in skour-
ginge ād correcting his owne people, as
in destroyinge his open enimies: it was
requisite that God shuld minister vnto
him sufficient power, for the accompli-
shment of his determinat counselle,
which the Lorde did in such abundance,
as no Nation was able to resiste him,
that shuld not perishe either with the
sworde of Nabuchadnezer, or famine,
either els in that the Lorde hí self would
from heauen fight on his parte withe
the plague of pestilence.

And of this what thing els gather we,
but firste the purpose of Ieremie: that
was to drawe the Iewes frō their follie,
which after they had once forsaken the
Lorde by rebellion, did thinke also by
their policie to escape Gods appoynted

punishmet. No no, woulde Ieremie say:
it is to late, and ye are to weake to fight
against the Lorde whose worke this is.
When ye were Lordes within your selues, and had full libertie to honor your
Lorde God, according to the Lawes whi
che he gaue vnto you, and whereby ye
were assured to lyue without feare of all
natiós, you wolde not. And therfore shall you serue a strange kinge, strange
lawes, and a stráge nation til you be wel
correcked ád humbled: till you haue felt
by experience what an inestimable có-
fort it is to haue the liuinge Lorde to be
your kinge ád gouernour. And therfor
woulde Ieré say, Serue Nabuchadnezer.

Seinge thé this is the appoynted plague of God for disobeyinge him and his
Lawes, to serue strange kinges, and to be
captiues. you are hereby warned ád taught, rather to turne with all spede to the
liuinge Lorde, and to set vp his true religió againe, that he may defend you: thé
in proceadinge in your blasphemye
for the cómandement and feare of any
creature, to hasten Gods wrath and Iu-
dgements. The Israelites because they
woulde not receaue the oft admonitiós
of

of Gods Pophetes to feare the Lord, co-
oulde not afterwarde escape his plagues,
nor the feare of men: no more shal you
(ô inhabiters of Englāde) without spee-
die repétance escape the Spaynishe plague of adoulterous Philippe whom the
Lorde will make his sworde and maul to
beate downe your townes and Cities, ād
to deuoure the people therof. For seinge
you haue with the Israelit s forsaké the   *Mans yo-*
swete ād plesant yoke of God and Chri   *ke is vn-*
ste his Sonne: you shal indure the impor   *supporta-*
table yoke of this cruell and beastly na-   *ble.*
tion.

But what, shall we obey then say you?
Yes verely: but against your wills in ca-
ptiuite and thraldom, as did the Israelites in Egypt and Babylon, to serue them
with your bodyes and goodes Seinge ye
woulde departe with nothinge to serue
our Maister and Sauiour Christ, thinke
you to escape this by obeyinge your
wicked Rulers? By what other means
haue you fallen into the handes of your
enemies, but by this kinde of obedience
onely? Whiche as you haue harde suffici
ently proued, is in Gods sight plaine disobedience and rebellion. But you

will say: Ieremie willed the Iewes to serue Nabuchadnezer which was a wicked
Prince, and then with out the feare of
God, and therfore are we bownd to serue our Quene, thoghe she be an vngodly idolatres? Ieremie speaketh but of
bodely seruice, and such as subiectes o-
we to their superiours in Ciuile ordinaunces, and outwarde doinges, and
not to defile their consciences in com-
mitting euill. For in suche thiges, both
God and his Prophetes, and the examples of all the godly do forbid all obediéce. They were made subiectes to the
kinge of Babylon to serue him with
their bodies and goodes, as were his o-
wne people: and also to paye tribute to
him as did strangers, which he had likewise subdued. The which thing was for
their punishment. And therfore of duetie they must patientlie beare them.

   Thé in fewe wordes I answere, that althoghe it be moste lawfull with patience to beare the punishment of the Lorde for our synne, and not to repine or
rebell agaynst it: yet is it our parte neuerthelesse, and bownden duety, to defende and mayntayne the cause of God
                with

What obe-
dience and
seruice Ie-
remie re-
quireth.

with all our might: and to whithstand all
maner of aduersaries, euen to the losse
of our goods and liues: being euer assured of this promesse of our Sauiour and
Maister, That he that loseth his liffe for
his sake, shall finde it: and he that loseth
father or mother, frindes or goodes in
his cause, shall be rewarded an hundreth
folde in this worlde, and in the worlde
to come with liffe euerlasting.

Mat.19.

It is not then wisedome to repine
at the rodde when it is layde vpon vs to
beate vs, but to returne backe to our
mercifull Father with vnfayned repentance, calling for mercy before hande
whiles he doth but menace vs. And therfore the threatning or counselle of Ieremie, is but an admonition for vs to o-
beye God in true religion whan we haue tyme: that therby we may escape the
like plagues: ãd no defẽce at all for our
vngodlie behauiour in yelding to the
deuilishe decrees of anie vngodly Magistrates, what names or titles soeuer
they beare. For this answere of the A-
postles must euer more preuaile: God
must be obeyed rather then man. And
there is no obedience in euil that can

*Godes pla-
gues oght to
moue vs to
repentance
and not to
harden vs
in euil.*

pleafe the almightie.

Laſte of all we haue to conſider the
The thirde ſainge and doinge of the worthie ſerua-
obtection. nte of God the kinge and Prophet Dauid, who woulde not lift vp his hand a-
1. Sa̅ 24 gainſte kinge Saule, notwithſtanding he
and. 49. ſought to haue murthered Dauid, ſaige:
God forbid that I ſhoulde touche the a-
noynted of the Lorde: and why? Becauſe
he is the anoynted of the Lorde. If it be
not lawfull the̅ to touche the kinge becauſe he is the Lordes anoynted : it is likewiſe vnlawfull to diſobey or reſiſte,
for that he is the Lords anoynted.

Anſwere To whiche I anſwere, that to conſider
the bare wordes, it woulde ſeeme true as
they ſay: but wayige the cauſe, the mat-
The cauſe ter is eaſie to anſwere. The occaſion wh-
why Da erfore Saul, hated Dauid, was for that he
uid was knewe he ſhould ſucceade him in his
hated of kingdome. As Saule him ſelfe doth con-
Saule. feſſe in the ſame Chapter, ſaynge: I knowe of a ſuertie that thou ſhalt reigne,
1. Sa. 24 and that the kingdom of Iſraell ſhal be
eſtabliſſhed in thy hande . Swere to me
therfore by the Lorde, that thou wilte
not cut of my ſeed after me, nor deſtroye
my name frome my fathers howſe. This
                                being

beinge thē Dauids owne priuate cause, *None oght to reuenge his owne priuate cause.* it was not lawfull for him in that case to seke his owne reuengemēt:especially in murtheringe violently his anoynted kinge,and the anoynted of the Lorde . For it is not written of Saule,that he was an idolatrer or constrayned his people to worshippe strange Godes,nor yet was aboute to sel thē to the enemies of God the Philistines, against whom he foghte manfully and many tymes. Nether that he was an open oppressor and cōtemner of the Lawes of God, as are this day all the rulers in miserable England . And therfore Dauid beinge but a priuate man, coulde haue done no violence to his kinge without Godes especial inspiratiō, except in reuēginge his priuat cause he had vsurped Gods office and soght to haue established him self in his kingdome,not taryige the Lords appoitmēt. *Rulers cōtemninge Gods lawes are as well*

But where as the kinges or Rulers are become altogether blasphemers of God , and oppressors and murtherers of their subiectes , then oght they to be accōpted no more for kinges or lawfull Magistrats, but as priuate mē: and to be examined, accused, condemned and punished by the Lawes of God, wherunto *subiect to the punishement of the same as priuat persōs.*

they are and oght to be ſubiect, and
being conuicted and puniſhed by that
Lawe, it is not mãs, but Gods doing: who
as he dothe appoynte ſuch Magiſtrates
ouer his people by his Lawe, ſo doth he
condemne aſwel them as the people trãſ
greſsing agaynſte the Lawe. For with
God ther is no reſpecte of perſones, as
here after folowith more largely.

Thus we ſee that althoghe Dauid
thoght it not lawful in his priuate cauſe
to touche Gods anoynted, yet are no
people or nation therby cõſtrayned either ot obeye their anoynted in vnlawful demandes, or els forbidden to withſtand the open tranſgreſsion of Gods
Lawes and mans. For in that caſe Saules
ſeruauntes would not obeye him, com-
mandinge them to murther Ahimelech
and the reſt of the Leuites ãd Prieſtes: ſo
that not to withſtand ſuch rages of Prin
ces in tyme according as the Lawe requireth (which commandeth that the
euill be taken forth from amõgeſt you)
is to geue them the bridle to all kynde
of miſchiffe, to ſubuerte all Lawes of
God and man, to let will rule for reaſon,
and therby to inflame Gods wrathe
agaynſt

1.Sam.22

Deu.17.

agaynſt you, wholy, as your ſelues in
Englande are this day an example to all
natiõs and people that beare the Name
of Chriſte.

These are the obiections for the mo
ſte parte, or at the leaſt the chiefeſt, which are comonly alleadged agaynſt this
veritie moſte playne and euidente : that
is that there is no obedience to be a-
lowed agaynſt God, which is not in his
ſight diſobedience. Also that it is lawfull for all men according to their vo-
catiõ to reſiſte to the vttermoſt of their
power all ſuch as are open enimies of
God, and labour to make them ſlaues to
Satan. Theſe obiections as you playnly
ſee, make nothing to the cõtrarie : but if
they ſhall be depely conſidered, do rather ſtrongly confirme the ſame. Therfore deare brethern, let no man feare to
ſhewe him ſelf Gods ſeruante openly,
and to forſake in tyme the ſhamefull
bõdage of Satan, to call back the trueth
of Gods worde agayne, wherby ye were
once in freedome both of conſciẽce and
bodie : and vtterly to aboliſhe all vile
papiſtrie the doctrine of deuils, and
onely cauſe of all your calamitie,

The obie-
ctions do
cleare this
doctrine
and noth-
inge dar-
ken it.

both of bodie and soule.

CHAP. XI.

It apperteyneth not onely to the Magistrates and al other inferior officers to see that their Princes be subiect to Gods Lawes, but to the comon people also: wherby the tyrannie of the Princes and rebellion of the subiects may be auoyded.

TO resiste euill and to mayntayne goodnesse, to honor God truely and to expel idolatrie, euery man will confesse to be a good and godly acte, ãd cannot but highlie commende the workers therof, as men acceptable to God, and worthie members of a comon welthe: but when men cõsider the daungers and displeasures, which commonly happen to such, then is there great curtesie made who first shall take the enterprise in hand: and longe disputations made whither it be their duetie or no: and to what sortes of men it doth belong, as thogh any were exempted out of that nomber which do professe the Name of God. If the superior power be an idolatrer or a cruel tyrant suppressing true religion and murthering the Sainctes of

God

God (as Iesabel of England doth with
all her rable of papistical Bishopps, and
shauelinges)who is so ignorant of God,
or destitute of all humanitie or natural
iudgment,that wil not aknowledge such
a one to be vnworthie the societie of
the godly and honest: muche lesse to
haue the auctoritie and rule ouer great
nations and whole kingdoms?

And not with out cause. For bythe
Ciuile Lawes, a foole or idiot borne,and
so proued,shall lose his landes and inhe-
ritance wherunto he is borne, because
he is not able to vse them a right: but es
pecially oght in no case to be suffered
to haue the regiment of a whole nation
or kingdome. And it is moste certeyne
that there is no such euil can come to a-
ny comon welth by fooles and idiots, as
dothe by the rage and furie of vngodly
Rulers, maynteyners of idolatrie ād tyrannie. For follie hath comonly ioyned
with it simplicitie, voyde of malice and
easie to be ordered:but idolatrie and ty
rānie reseblethmore the nature of wilde
beastes, cruell beares,ād ragig lyós, thē
the códicion of mā.For simplicitie,they
are replenished with craftines:for loue,

*The gou-
uernemēt
of fooles
more tole
rable then
of tyrants.*

they shew malice: and for patience, furious rage ād madnesse and beinge borne as it were a comō plague to all men, cannot once studie for the preseruation of a fewe.

This besides reason, experience teacheth all men to be moste true, that it were better to haue anie foole, thē such an vntamed beaste to be ouer thē. And that suche being altogether with out God, oght to haue no auctoritie ouer the people of God, who by his worde requireth the contrarie as is moste manifeste. And yet to punishe, and depose such a one according to the commandemēt of God, there is none that thinketh *Deu. 17.* it Lawfull: or at the least will confesse it to appertayne vnto them, either to do it them selues, or to see it done by others. As for the wicked counsellers, they are *Suche as* playne Gnatos and flatterers, thinking *onelye flat-* their office to be applyed vnto their ki-*tter the* ges and Quenes will, as thogh they had *appetites of* no charge of the whole Realme. And *their prin* therfore will labour to cōpasse nothīge *ce.* but that which their Princes lust after, or may at the least please them, not passing if the whole Realme do perishe, so they

they maye obtayne their fauours. Suche, Achitophels deſerue to haue Achitophels rewarde, for their deuiliſhe coūſelle with out mercie. And as it is with them, ſo is it with the reſte of all eſtates, as before hath bene touched. Neuertheleſſe, the matter is ſo euident vpon their partes, that all will cōfeſſe that it chiefly belōgeth to inferior Magiſtrats to ſee a redreſſe in ſuch diſordres: and they thē ſelues can not well deny it.

But as touching the comon and ſymple people, they thinke them ſelues vtterly diſcharged, whither their Prince be godlie or vngodlye, wiſe or fooliſhe, a preſeruer of the comon welthe or ells a diſtroyer, all is one to them, they muſte be obedient, becauſe they are ignorant, and muſte be led them ſelues, not meete to leade others. And becauſe their doinges are counted tumultes and rebellion (except they be agreable to the commandmentes, decrees, and proceadinges of their ſuperior powers and Magiſtrates, and ſhal in doing the contrary be as rebells puniſhed) therfore of all others (ſay they) we haue leaſt to do, yea nothing at all withe the doinges of our

The vaine excuſe of the cōmū people.

k.

Rulers. Yf they rule well, we fhall fare
the better : if they be vngodly they haue the more to anfwere for their vngodlyneffe . What haue we to do with their
matters? Thus do all fortes of men from
the higheft to the loueft flyppe their
heades out of the coller : and as careles
perfones not pafsing which end goeth
forwarde , geueth the brydle wholie to
their Rulers till deftruction remediles
oue rflowe all.

To the intent therfore that this fim-
plicitie, ignoráce, and fubiection of the
inferior people, do not altogether blynde them, and caufe them (as hitherto it
hath bene proued almoft in all places
and countries) to fuffer them felues like
brute beaftes rather then reafonable
creatures , to be led and drawen where
fo euer their Princes commandementes
haue called : either to arme them felues
agaynft Chrift their Sauiour in ouerthro
wing the truthe of his Gofpel to bringe
in Antichrifte and papiftrie: or els to fy-
ght agaynft their owne brethern the fer
uátes of God, to robbe them, expel them
out of their one howfes, poffefsions and
countrie , to torment them and cruelly
                                          put

put them to death: as thoghe the cōman
dement of the Prince coulde make that
lawfull, which God forbiddeth as deteſtable: as thoghe they being made in-
ſtruments to their Princes in executing
vngodly tyrannie, ſhulde not be parta-
kers likewiſe with thē of Gods vengeāce
in the daye of his dreadfull viſitatiō, whē
nether their ignorāce can excuſe, them,
nether cōmandement of kinge or Prince defende thē, but they workinge wick-
edneſſe with their Rulers ſhall drinke
of the ſame cup with them alſo.

Ignorance can not exeuſe the people.

To theintent (I ſaie) that they ſhulde be no more ſo blynded, nor runne
headlonge (as they do) to their owne deſtruction: I haue thoght good moreouer
and beſides that which hitherto hathe
bene ſpoken in general (wherof notwithſtanding they might alſo gather
what belongeth to them in their condicion and eſtate) to ſhewe vnto them more eſpecially what may be demanded
of comon people by Gods worde, and
what the people alſo may lawfully
deny to do by the ſame worde of God.
Which as it oght to be permitted and
preached to all men in general: ſo

shulde it be the comon and onely rule
wherby to frame and ordre all mens
liues and doinges.

And to auoyde all incomodities
that are accustomed to happen in all comon welthes, as wel vpon the Magistrats
parte as of the people, there are two ex-
tremities: wherof bothe muste be warned. The first is, that the Magistrates per
mit not to their subiectes ouermuche
libertie, least therby they fall in to contempte and subiection of their people:
wherof folowethe for the moste parte,
all kynde of dissolutnesse, ād carnall libertie, subuertió of all good Lawes and
ordres, alteracion of common welthes
and policies, contempt of God and man:
and to be shorte, all thinges turned
to disorder and confusion. The seconde
apparteyneth on the other parte, to the
people, which oght not to suffer all
power and libertie to be taken from
them, and therby to become brute beastes, with out iudgmente and reason,
thinking all thinges lawfull, which
their Rulers do with out exceptió, commāde them, be they neuer so farre from
reason or godlynesse: as thoghe they
were

Two extre
mities to
be auoy-
ded.
To muche
libertie is
not to be
permitted
to the peo-
ple.

The liber-
tie of the
people.

were not reaſonable creatures, but brute beaſtes: as thoghe there were no difference betwixt bonde ſlaues, and free
ſubiectes: and as thoghe they had no
portió or right at all in the coútrie where they inhabite: but as they were altogether created of God to ſerue their kin
ges and gouernors like ſlaues, and not
their kings & gouernors appoynted of
God to preſerue his people, wher of they
are but a portion and members, albeit
they occupie the cheif roume ád office,
not to bringe the reſt of the members in
cótempte and bondage, but to comforte them, defende them, and noriſhe them
as members of the ſame bodie.

And as the people may be aſſured by
Gods worde that this libertie apparteyneth to them, which becommeth members of one bodie and brethern, becauſe
the Lorde God him ſelf (from whom kin
ges haue their auctoritie and power) cal Deu. 17.
leth their ſubiectes and people their *Subiectes*
brethern, charging them in no caſe to *oght not to*
lift them ſelues aboue them, but as bret- *ſuffer thē*
hern to rule in all humbleneſſe and loue *ſelues to be*
ouer them: euenſo, the people, if they *made*
ſuffer this right to be taken from them, *ſlaues.*

which God of his singuler fauour hath
graunted. then are they an occasió that
their kiges and Rulers are turned to tyrantes, and cruel oppressors, according
as Samuel promised the people of Israel
shulde come vpon them, insomuche as
they had refused his gouernement, who
ruled ouer them, in all iustice, and hum-
blenesse, and in such sorte as no man
coulde charge him with any crime. And
therfore the Scriptures pronounce that
they reiected not Samuel, but God him
self i whose feare he ruled. This (saith Sa
muel) shal be the Lawe of the kige, which shallrule ouer you. Your childré shall
he take to serue in his chariot, and to be
his horse men, and they shall runne before his chariot, and he shall constitute
also Captayns of a thousand, and of
fiue hundreth, and others to till his gro-
wnde, and to gather his harueste, to make weapons for warre, and harnesse for
his chariots. Moreouer, he shall take
your daughters to make his anoynt-
méts, to serue his kitchin, and to be his
clothiers: besides this he shall take your
fyeldes and your vineyardes, your be-
ste orchardes of oliues and geue to his
seruaunts, and of your corne and vines

1. Sam 8

The descri-
ption of a
wicked
kinge and
tyrante.

shall he take the tenthes, and geue them
to his Eunuches, and seruauntes: your
seruauntes also and maydes and the
chif of your youthe and your asses, shall
he take to do his worke. And of your
cattell shall he take the tenth, and you
shall become his seruauntes: and you
shall crye out that day in the sight of
your kinge whom you haue chosen, and
the Lorde God will not heare you that
day: and why? Bycause they had rather
haue a kinge and Ruler of their owne ap
poyntment, then of the Lordes.

Wherfore to auoyde the daungers
vpon both partes, it is more then necessarie that bothe be subiecte to that Rule, and with all diligent care, labour to
reteyne it, wherby both maye learne
their duetie, and be constrayned iustly
to execute the same. For when the comon people and subiectes haue so large libertie by the negligence of their
Rulers, that customes and vnlawful v-
sages shall be preferred to Gods Lawes,
and statutes, and that to maynteyne
the same customes, they care nothing
if all other good Lawes, either of God
or man, do perishe: how is it possible

*Both Ma-
gistrates
and cōmōs
oght to o-
bey Gods
Lawes.*

without daungerous tumultes, and rebel
lion, to brynge them to any good ordre
and reformation, except there be some
comon, and approued Lawe, which verie
nature, and the feare of God will teach
them to reuerence, and obeye? As for ex
ample : amongs other customes which
mayntayne idlenes, and serue the greedy appetite of the bellie (which all men
are loth to forgo) how harde a thinge
kinge Ed- were it to bryng them frome their San-
warde de ctes dayes? The abolishment wherof,
sierous godly king Edwarde in his tyme coulde
that God not bryng to passe. So great was the nom
shuld ha- ber of Papistes in the Perlament house,
ue had his which maiteyned those superstitiouse da
due honour yes, some bearig the name of mé, ad so-
sowght me of womé, ascrybig that to the creatu
the abolish res of God, which apperteyneth to him
ment of all alone, for as muche as euery day is the
Sainctes Lordes worke, and oght to serue to his
dayes. honour onely. They haue nowe in tyme
of papistrie, dayes of Peter and Paule,
All. dayes Marie, and Iohn, withe the reste of the
are the Apostles: they haue Georges daye, and
Lordes ã i katherines, Dunstans day the coniu-
onelye ap rer, and Loye the smithe, with innume-
pertayne rable others, which maynteyne the idle-
vnto him nesse

nesse of them and of their seruaunts
contrarie to the ordinaunce of God, ap-
poynting six dayes for their trauell, and
the seuenth daye onely to reste , and
that to the honoring of our Lorde God.

Also by what means may the people be drawen from the dayes of riote
and bancketing, which they terme frind-
ly feasting and goodfelloweshipp: as
from Whitsontides dronkennes and sur-
fet, Midsomers shewes and vanities,
Christmas riote and bawdry , Shrofte-
twesdayes glottony, and Lents supersti-
tious obseruations, excepte by some Lawe of greater importance, the rude peo
ple be otherwise perswaded? And what
other Lawes are there able to bringe
this to passe besides the Lawes of God?
Wherin if they be not instructed , it is
impossible for any auctoritie or power to withholde them, with out great
daunger and tumultes from such kinde of disordres and vnlawfull customes.

Therfore if thou be a Ruler and co-
uete to haue the people obedient to
thee in Gods feare, this muste be thy
first and principall studie to, procure

Sainctes days with the seruice appointed vnto them oght by Gods worde to be abolished.

How harde a thing it is to alter euil customes.

The meanes to breake euil customs.

that they may truely know God by the playne and diligent preaching of his worde, wherſ if they be well inſtructed, there is no cuſtome ſo longe continued, no idleneſſe ſo longe vſed, no ſuperſticion ſo deeply rooted, which they will not gladly and peaceably for go at thy commandement: yea, there is no thing which is euill, that they can for ſhame ſtandein: nor any good and lawfull demande, that they will deny thee. By theſe means onely ſhalt thou obtayne honour, maintayne thy right, winne the hartes of thy people, and haue them all obedient.

And as the Magiſtrates by this means, are ſure to finde obedience, and eſcape all rebellion, tumultes and diſordres amonges their ſubiectes: euenſo is there no other rule for the ſubiectes to eſcape the idolatrie, tyrannie, and oppreſsion of their ſuperiors, then in reteyning (as their chief poſſeſsion) the ſelf ſame Lawe and worde of God. Permitting rather all thinges wordlie to be taken from them, as landes, goodes, houſe, cōtrie, father, mother, wiffe, children, yea liffe it ſelf, then to be depriued

ued by any means of that heauenly trea
sure and precious perle, for the which
they must sell althinges. Wherof to be
fullie perswaded, it is necessary to vnderstande what maner of people you
are.

Mat. 13,

Yf you be the people of God, and vnfayned Christians, then muste ye also
knowe that the Lawe of God, and
Christe your Sauiour, doth appertayne
vnto you: wherin, as without shame ād
condemnation ye may not be ignorāt:
euenso no power, commandment, or
threatninges, shulde cause you to departe from it, wherin onely standethe
that comforte and saluation, which no
creature can restore agayne vnto you.

what trea
sures God
hath com-
mitted to
the charge
of his
people.

The heathen which knewe not God
a right, but were idolatrers, yet made
their religiō to haue the highest place in
their comon welthes: as Aristotle writeth in his Politiques. In the name wherof they might demande any thinge
of their kinges and Rulers, and they
durst not denye them: and might also
with out offence deny all thinges which their Rulers demaunded contrarie
to their religion. In so muche as this

prouerbe was comon amongeſt all , *vſ-que ad Aras* : meaning that agaynſt their religion (as they were perſwaded) they were bownde to no perſone: father, mother, frende, or gouernour: their loue ãd obedience towardes thé coulde ſtretch no further then to the Altars , that is, ſo farre as with obſeruing their religion, they might lawfullye performe.

Yf the Gentills then had their religion in ſuch honour and reuerence that agaynſt it (thoghe in dede it was meere ſuperſtition and idolatrie) they woulde acknowledge no obedience: in what eſtimation ſhulde Gods worde and the religion of our Sauiour Ieſus Chriſte be amongeſt vs that profeſſe his Name, and are aſſured of his doctrine to be the vndouted trueth and power of God to ſaluacion of all beleuers ? Yf the heathen kinges and Magiſtrates coulde cõpell their ſubiectes no farther then the Alters : ſhall any auctoritie or power compell vs farther then God , and his anoynted our chief kinge, Lorde ãd Maiſter? Let it be counted ſhame to vs, that the ignorant Gentils ſhuld be founde more carefull and zelous in defending their

In what reuerence we oght to haue Gods worde.

their superstition and manifeste idolatrie, then we are in mayntayning the
true worship of God and his heauenly
wisedome.

Yf we were Turkes, Sarasins, Iewes
or papistes, which either knewe notGod
a right, or els denied his Sonne Iesus: it
were no great maruell if we were led
after the lustes of our vngodly Princes.
For as our Maister teacheth, When the
blynde leadeth the blynde, bothe fall   Mat.15.
in to the diche.But if we will be taken
for the people of God and his sonnes by
adoption in Christ Iesus, then it behoueth vs likewise to geue obediéce, prin-
cipally to our Lorde and Maister, to our
mightie God and moste louinge Father,
as Malachi the Prophet exhorteth. The
sonne reuerenceth the father, and the   Mala.1.
seruaút the maister: yf I be your Father
(saith the Lorde) where is the honor
that you geue me? Yf I be your Lorde
and Maister where is my feare?Notinge
vnto vs how it is in vayne to call him
Father or Lorde, so long as we geue him
not that honour and reuerence which
he demandeth.

Also, if we will not be taken for

blynde and ignorante perſones, then muſt we ſhewe forth this light by walking as becomethe the childré of light, as the Apoſtle requirethe indifferently of all Gods children with out exceptió, or excuſe either of guide or Ruler. For the blyndneſſe of our guide, whither he be of the Cleargie or Laytie may be no excuſe to vs, if in folowing him we fall and periſhe: it is our owne faute, and we muſt beare our owne iudgment. For Chriſte hereof admoniſheth vs: Let thé a lone (ſaithe he) for they are blind guides, and leaders of the blynd. And agayne, accordinge to their workes, ſee ye do not.

Ephe.5.
Iohn.12.

Mat 15.

Mat.23.

Yf thou hauynge ſight, had appoynted to thee a blynde guide, wouldeſte thou folowe him into a daungerouſe pit or deepe water, wherin both might periſhe becauſe he was thy guide? Then truely mighteſt thou be iudged of all men worſe then either oxe or aſſe, or any other vnreaſonable beaſte, whiche will not be driué in ſuch places, as to their outwarde ſéſes appeare daúgerous.

Nature onely teacheth all creatures this, to flie frome thoſe daungers that ſhulde

shulde hurte them: and to desier all thinges that do them good. And when God hath made this comon to all beastes, ād inferior creatures, paynefully to seeke their preseruation: hathe he denied the same to man, whome aboue all others he will haue preserued? For whose preseruation chieflie he hath not onely created all thiges and prescribed his Lawes and commandements to prohibet murther, and euery other thinge tendinge to his destruction: but also to shewe the abundance of his mercies, spared not his dearelye belouid Sonne, but gaue him to the cruell death of the Crosse, that man might haue full saluation, not onely here in this world, but euerlastingly in the worlde to come.

Nature teacheth to flee hurtful thinges

God hath created all thinges for mans commodite

Wherfore, if he tender vs so muche, as to seeke by all meās possible our liffe and preseruation, then must it likewise followe, that he hath constitute no lawes, or ordinances to our destruction, so longe as we shall be founde obedient vnto them. Then is there no power that ruleth accordinge to these lawes, which either can or will cōmande vs anie thige, tēdinge to our destructiō. But if anie

Tobi.3.
Esai.3.

so do by Gods permiſſion becauſe of our ſynnes, ād rebellion towardes him (for which cauſe onelie he ſuffreth wicked Princes to be our Gouernours) it is (deare brethren) to drawe vs to repentaunce, and knowledge of our ſynnes, and not that we ſhulde forſake the Lawes of our God, and to contynew in our wonted rebellion, by yelding to the vngodlie commandments of wicked men.

CHAP. XII.

¶How muche the comon people owe to God for his benefits receaued, what obedience he requirethe, how farre they are charged, what thinges they haue promiſed, and how ignoraunce maye not excuſe them.

 LL theſe thinges being well conſidered, it is an eaſie matter for all maner of ſubiectes to knowe what libertie belongeth vnto them, by the worde of God, whiche they maye lawfullie clayme, as their owne poſſeſſió, and are likewiſe bounde at all tymes to practiſe: wherin alſo appeareth what thinges are prohibited ynto them, whiche

che they maye in no cafe exercife. Yf
you therfore be Gods fubiectes and
people, and he your Lorde God and louinge Father, who is aboue all powers
ād Princes, ād hath made no Lawes, but
fuch as are for your preferuation, and
finguler comforte: then without all
controuerfie there maye be nothinge
lawfull for you by anie commandment
of man, whiche your Lorde God in anie
cafe forbiddeth: and nothinge vnlawfull
or forbidden to you whiche he commandeth, whither it appartayne to the
firfte Table or the Seconde. Which rule A rule for
all to obfer
ue.
if ye obferue, you maye be affured to
pleafe God: likeas by doinge the contrarie, ye fhall purchafe his heauie wrathe and indignation. For no mā can ferue two Maifters at once: but he fhall hate the one, ād loue the other. And in ha- Mat. 6.
tinge your firfte and chief Lorde to o-
beye and pleafe man, beholde your impietie is intolerable, prefarringe vile mā
his creature, to the Almightie God and
creator of all.

How muche we are bownde to hisMa-
ieftie, our owne confcience doth beare
vs witneffe: whiche can not deny but

that we haue receauid of him alone our
liffe mouing and being, our wiſedome
ſtrégthe, bewtie, riches, childré, ãd allthí
ges that are good ãd profitable, inwhoſe
power we may do all thíges, ãd with out
hí all fleſhe is turned to duſt ãd powder.

Pſ.1.7.17

Remember the example of the worthie Captayne and Prince Moyſes, whó
God choſe to delyuer his people from
Egypt, who woulde not charge thé with
anie thinge at any tyme whiche the Lor
de his God had not commanded, euer-
more ſpeakinge on this wiſe, Theſe are
the ſtatutes and preceptes of the Lorde:
Thus ſayth the Lorde : and, Heare ô
Iſrael the voyce of the Lord, &c. In ſo
muche, as he had this for his onlie ſhil-
de agaynſte the murmuring people: It is
not agaynſt Aaron and me that ye mur-
mure but againſt the Lorde: which beíg
choſen and appoynted of the Lorde, did
onely execute his will and commandementes. Yea, as for them ſelues they có-
feſſed that they were nothinge. As for vs
(ſayde Moyſes) what are we? meaninge
but earth ãd aſſhes, the creaturs of God,
nothinge differinge from others, ſauing
for that auctoritie, wherunto they were
called,

Moyſes cha
rged hys
with no-
thinge that
God had
not com-
manded.

Exod.19.
Deu.4.20

called, ãd the obediéce which they she
wed in executige not their owne willes,
but the will and pleasure of God . And
why? but because they knew they were
the people of God with whó they were
charged, and beinge his people , how it
behoueth them to be ruled by no other
Lawes and ordinances , then by such as
God had geuen them.

Wherfore if Moyses and Aaron, Gods
electe and chosen seruants had no more
power ouer the people then his expresse
comandement permit, and that the peo
ple so far and no farther were bownd to
obeye them: how can we assure our selues that we offende not Gods Maiestie,
whose people we woulde be called, whé
witheout his worde , yea cótrary to his
expresse cómandemét we satisfie the re-
questes and statutes of vngodly rulers?

For as Moyses coulde cómande nothíge but fró the mouthe of the Lorde: so
coulde the people obey nothing but
that whiche proceaded from his mouthe also : aswell because they were his
people, as for that they had so promised
with one voyce and consent before God
ãd Moyses , whé the Lorde commanded

Deut. 10

Godes peo-
ple must
be gouer-
ned onely
by Gods
Lawes.
Exod. 19 .

him to say on this wise to the people.
You haue seene what I haue done to the
Egyptians, and how I haue caried you
vpon the winges of Egels, and led you
forthe to me. Yf therfore ye will diligét-
lye heare my voice, and obserue my cómandement, you shalbe my propre people before all nations : For myne is the
earthe. And you shalbe vnto me a kyn-
gely Priesthod , and an holy people.
Whiche wordes when Moses had pronounced before the whole people, they all

The people promiss. to God and Moses.

to gether with one accord, áswered: Whatsoeuer the Lorde shall speake , that
will we do . And Moyses praised them
(or God rather by moyses) sainge, They
did well in so answering . And therfore

Deu. 18.

promised to rayse them vp a Prophet like to him, &c. And this was the couenant onlye that God made with them
before he gaue them the Lawe in wry-
tinge , and the promes that they made
to obserue the same Lawe, that they mi
ght therby be his deare and chosen
people.

This example ought neuer to departe from the eyes of all such as are,
or woulde be Gods people . Wherin as
in a

in a moſt clere glaſſe it dothe appeare
how they are bownd to God , what
God requireth of them, and what they
haue promiſed to him . For as the Lorde God required nothinge of the Iſraelits , but that whiche was their duetie
to do, and he by his exceadinge benefits
in delyueringe them from their enimies had well deſerued: euenſo he byn-
deth thé to nothinge, but to obeye him.
Nether did they promiſſe anie farther,
ſaynge: We will do all thinges (not what
Moyſes or Aaron or anie other after
them ſhall of them ſelues commande)
but whatſoeuer our Lorde God ſhall
ſpeake, that will we do . More then this
God required not, nether were they
bownde any farther but to the Lawes
of God onely, whiche they promiſed
for them and their poſteritie to obſer-
ue. And God for that cauſe bleſſed them
aboue all nations , with his vnſpeakable benefits.

 So are we no leſſe bownde to obeye
the ſelf ſame God of Iſrael, whom we
alſo profeſſe in Chriſte Ieſu our Moyſes
and Captayne, by whom we are not o-
nely delyuered from bodely ſeruitude,

All chriſti-
ans are no
leſſ bonde
to obey
God and
his Law-
es, then
were the
Iſraelits

l. iii.

but from the moste vile and dangerous bondage of Satan through synne our spirituall enemie. To this worthiest delyuerer also haue we in Baptisme promised no lesse, yea, muche more obedience: because of the more abundance of graces, which by him we haue receaued. And besides this are moste straightly charged so to do. Not by the voyce of anie earthly creature, but by the mouth of God the Father speakinge frō the heauens: This is my dearely beloued Sonne, in whom I am delited, heare him: whose fidelitie also no lesse passed the faithfullnesse of Moyses, then did his honor and dignitie: being the Sonne of God, and promysed Sauiour, doing nothing at all, nor teaching any thing which his heuenly Father had not appoynted him to do and to teache.

Wherfore, as the Iewes had the Lawe of God and his commandementes for a sufficient dischaige agaynst all contrarie commandementes, of what auctoritie so euer they were, being no farther bownde to any creature thē the self same Lawes of God approued: euenso, all such as beare the Name of Christ and woulde be taken for the people of God,

Mat. 4. 17

thoghe they be of the baseſt ād loweſte
ſtate of ſubiectes, are no farther bownd
to any Prince or ſuperior power, nor
to their commandementes, then the cōmandement of the chief kinge ād Lorde
doth approue ād permitte, nor then their
promeſſe agayne to him doth require.

The cōmā dement of Princes cā not bynd vs contrary to Gods worde.

Nether may it be a ſufficiēt diſcharge for thee to alleadge ignorāce, becau
ſe thou art a ſubiecte, and therfore haſt
nothing to do, to inquire of the doinges
or to examyne the commandementes of
thy ſuperiors or Rulers, but wilt ſay with the multitude, If they commāde well
thou art obedient, if otherwiſe thou art
excuſed in doing as thou art cōmanded,
and they onely haue to anſwer to God
by whō thou art thus charged. Deſceaue
not thy ſelf (deare brother) For aſwell
art thou charged by Gods worde to kno
we what they commande thee, and not
to do it except it be lawfull, as they are
charged by their office to will nothīg of
thee, which Gods worde approueth not.
For as they in commanding ād doing e-
uill, ſhall not eſcape Gods heauy wrathe and iudgmētes : no more ſhalt
thou, being made an iuſtrument of

The vngodly opinion of the cōmō people.

As wel the obeyer of wickednes as the commāder ſhal be puniſhed.

l. iiii.

their impietie and vngodlyneffe. Therfore to be ignorant in rhefe thinges, althogh thou be a fubiecte, is to contemne the commandement of God, and to
neglecte thine owne faluation: for as
muche as God hath charged thee beinge one of his people, with the fame Lawes
(the Ceremonies except) wherwithe he
charged his people Israel before, and
willith thee no leffe to knowe his preceptes, and to obeye them, then he wil-
Deu.6.11 led the Ifralites. Of them he required
to haue his Lawes wryté vpon their do-
res and poftes, to inftructe their children in the fame, to talke of them fit-
ting at home, and when they walked in
the waye, when they went to bed, and
why the whé they fhuld rife. But to thee befides
Chriftiás all this, God hath fent a more fhining
oght grea light, our Sauiour Iefus Chrifte: which
ter obedi- euery man may clerely beholde, exce-
ence to Go pte he be wilfully blynde with the ftub-
ds worde berne Iewes. He is the light that fhine-
thé did the the in darkneffe, and lightneth euery
Iewes. man that commeth in to this worlde.
Ioh 1. He hathe taken away the fhaddoues ád
Ceremóies of the Lawe, that thou mayft
clerely beholde the will of his Father.
He

He hath vncouered Moyfes face, to the- Exol 34. 2 Cor 3.
intent thou mayft fully confider the fe-
crets of God. For thefe are the dayes
wherof the Prophet Ioel fpake, when all Ioel.2. Efai.44. Act.2.
fhulde be Prophets, and fee vifiõs. And it
fhal come to paffe in the latter dayes
(faith God) that I wil powre furth my
Spirite vpõ all flefhe, ãd your fonnes ãd
daughters fhall prophecie, your younge
men fhall fee vifions, and your auntients
fhall dreame dreames. And moreouer v-
pon my feruauntes and handemaydes
in thofe dayes, wil! I powre my Spirite,
and they fhall prophecie . Which pro- Act.2.
phecie. S. Peter affirmeth to be fulfilled
in the kingdome of Chrifte, where all
thinges are as playne and euident to all
fortes of men and women, which profef-
fe Chrifte vnfaynedly, as before his tyme they were to the Prophets them felues, or to fuch as God appeared vnto in
dreames or vifions.

And therfore, if ignorance of Gods
Lawes coulde not excufe the Iewes befo
re Chriftes commyng, which were con-
tynualy fubiecte to the punifhment of
God for their tranfgreffions (thoghe ma
ny thinges were obfcure as in fhadowes

and figures: how muche leſſe cá it excuſe any má now in ſo great lyght of the
Goſpel? Seing then thou knoweſt thy
ſelf bownd to obeye thy Lorde God a-
boue all others, becauſe of the ineſtima
ble benefits thou haſt receaued of him
in Chriſte Ieſus, and becauſe he requireth the ſame of thee, and thou haſt alſo
promiſed no leſſe to him in thy baptiſ-
me and profeſsion: and laſt of all in that
thou caneſt not pretende ignorance in
ſuch knowledge and ſhyninge bright-
neſſe, nor yet eſcape Gods vengeance,
which he with out reſpecte of perſones
wil powre indifferently vpon all tranſgreſſors, be they ſuperior powers, or
inferior ſubiectes. It is thy parte then,
beíg a ſubiecte, to learne this leſſon of
the Apoſtles (whé ſo euer thou ſhuldeſt
be conſtrayned, by commandement or
force of tyrantes to do euill) That God
muſt be obeyed before man. Which vnto thee wil be as ſufficiét a defence and
buckler in all aſſaultes and daungers, as
it is to all other ſortes of men in auctoritie and office: as was before declared.

Both hie ád lowe muſt learn this leſſon of the Apoſtels.

Art thow then, being a ſubiecte com-
maúded to worſhipp ſtockes and ſtones
which

which this day to our shame are ere- *Idols for*
cted agayne in Englande? Beholde thou *the true*
haft Gods commandement for thy de- *God.*
fence: Thou shalt commit no idolatrie,
nor make to thy self any grauen image *Exod. 20.*
&c. Art thou charged to be at the idola- *Deu. 5.*
trous Masse, wherin Christe thy Lorde
is blasphemed? Beholde, he hath geuen *The abo-*
thee an other charge: that is, to celebra- *minable*
te his Supper, according as he left in ex- *masse for*
ample, sayng: Do you this, that is, which *the holy*
ye se me do, ad not which the powers of *Supper of*
the worlde, or the pestilét papistes com- *the Lorde.*
mande. Also do it (saith Christe) in re- *Mat. 26*
membrance of me, and not of your frin- *Cōparison*
des alyue or departed, as teache the Pa- *betwixt*
pistes. For none of thé died for you. Mo- *the masse*
re ouer do it to shewe forth the deathe *and the*
of Christe, til his coming, as witnesseth *Lordes Su*
the Apostle: and not to make a new sa- *pper.*
crifice for synne, as the Papists blasphe- *I. Cor. 11*
mously both teache and preache. Art
thou commanded by men to disho-
nour the Sabbathe day in worship- *How the*
ping of Sainctes and abstayning v- *Sabbath*
pon their dayes and euens from thy *is abused.*
lawfull busines? Beholde, God thy
Lorde chargeth thee no further then
onely with his daye of reste, saying:

See thou keepe holie the Sabbath of the
Lorde thy God: and not of Peter, Paule,
Marie, Iames or Iohn. Art thou commãded to sweare in the name of Marie and
all the Sainċts in heauen? (which is the
papistical othe) Beholde, the Lorde saithe, Thow shalt onely sweare in the Name of thy Lorde and God. Art thou com
manded not onely to take the Name of
the Lorde in vayne, but also to forswere
thy self moste shamefully agaynst Gods
glorious Maiestie, and the honor of our
Sauiour Christe? (as all they haue done
which lately haue sworne to acknowledge Antichriste the bloudy butcher of
Rome to be their head and gouernour)
Beholde, The Lorde will not suffer his
house vnpunished that taketh his Name in vayne: muche lesse such periured
and forsworen wretches. Art thou commanded to persecute thy parentes and
frendes, charged not to succour them in
their necessitie, because they professe
the doctrine of saluation? Art thow forbidden lawfull mariage, because thou
art a minister of Gods worde, and permitted to lyue in all kinde of filthie vn-
clennesse, as do the Sodomiticall Priestes

To swear
by Saincts
is contrarie
to Gods
worde.
Deut. 6. 10
Iosua. 23.
Esai 45.

stes, Môkes, Freers, Nónes, Cardinales, Deanes, Archdeacons, and all other other orders of Satan : beholde such dothe the Lorde God as most abominable of all other, cômâde to be put to death.

Leu.20.

To be shorte, when they contrarie to their othe and profession, commande thee to receue Antichriste, the beastlie Bishoppe of Rome, with all his filthie dregges of damnation: to burne the worde of God and the faithfull interpreters and professers of the same: to forgo the comfortable preaching of the Gospel, and reading of the Scriptures: to persecute Christe in his mébers: to ayde the enimies with thy goods and bodie agaynst the deare childré of God: to fight in other countries with out any iuste cause or occasion, and to suffer thy wiffe, children, kinsfolkes and countryemen to be moste cruelly spoyled, oppressed and murthered for want of thy defence at home (as they most shamfully haue done of late, which at the cômandement of that cruell tyrât, prepared them selues to fight agaynst the Fréche kinge, and their owne brethern the Skottes, whiles the Spaniards put

The sume of Antichrists doctrine

Vnlawful warres.

Oh lamétable mi. serie.

them selues in a redinesse to entre the
Realme and make a generall spoyle and
pray of all.

These thinges and many such like are playnly forbidden you by the
manifest worde of God: and therfore to
do them for feare or pleasure of anie
Prince or power, is playne disobedience
and rebellion agaynst the Almightie.
And contrariewise, to answere in this
case, and to do as the Apostles haue
taught, that is, to obeye God rather
then man, is the onely waye to discharge your cósciences, to do your dueties,
and to please God: no more to be made
by ignorance the instrumentes of his
sworen enimies (what title so euer they
beare)to subuerte Gods glorie, oppres-
se your brethern, and distroye your
countrie: but repenting your former i-
gnorance and impietie, to be made instrumentes of thecontrarie to the vttermost of your power, least you be taken
in your synne, and preuented with the
bitter cup of Gods indignatió, alreadie
prepared for the workers of iniquitie,
and all such, as are ayeders, and parta-
kers with them, when nether power can
defend the superiors, nor their com-

mandmentes, excuse the subiectes.

CHAP. XIII.

The redinesse of the people to defende idolatrie, superstition, and earthly commodities: and their slouthfulnesse in maynteyning the cōtrarie How they are charged to see the Lawes of God kept, and the transgression of the same punished, if their rulers do neglecte them. And that they may lawfully punish their Magistrates as priuate persones transgressing the Lordes precepts.

BVt what remedie? (saye you) we being but subiectes with out power, ād wisedome cannot helpe it. The more pyttie deare Countriemen, that you haue so stoutly or rather stubbernely shewed your willes and power in the dayes of Godly kynge Edwarde the VI. your late Prince and gouernour, and the zelous seruant of God: who soght to rule you in Gods feare, ād vnder whom you had the consortable worde of God, ād were deliuered from the Romishe Antichrist, and from all superstition, for the most parte, hauing your Realme free from strangers, and quiete from all enimies, enioying your goods and freinds in peace with out all force.

Rebellion against the lawful gouernement of godly kinge Edwarde ād obedience to the vniuste vsurpation of wicked Marie.

imprisóning, reuilig, banishing, or mur
thering) It is to be lamented (I saye)
that then receauing all these blessinges of God, by the means of so worthie
a Prince, ye were able to conspire, rise
and rebell with the daunger of bodies,
goods and soules, agaynst your godlie
and lawfull kinge : and that chiefly to
defende the deuilishe Masse, and all the
puddels of poperie with the Caterpil-
lers and rable of all vncleane spirites, as
Cardinalls, Bishopps, Priestes, Monkes,
Freers, Nonnes &c. And now in these
matters wherin consisteth the glorie
of God, the preseruation of your owne
liues, and defence of your countrie
you are without all will, power and
helpe.

Reu.16.

 To restore Antichrist agayne, whom
ons God had banished to all your com-
fortes, you were not ashamed to terme
it obedience, and to counte your selues
therin no rebells, but lawfull resisters:
but to defende Christe and his confortable Gospell (which then you had in
possession) that are you persuaded to be
open rebellion. To arme your selues a-
gaynst your superiors, to defend your
comons

How sure
mans iugd
ment diffe
reth from
Gods.

cómons and earthly commodities with
holden from you, by the greedy desier
of new vpstarte gentlemen, how willing and redie haue you shewed your
selues? But to holde and reteyne your
spiritual possession not promised onely, but geuen in to your handes, you are
moste slowe without all hope and courage. Shall not this be to your iuste con
demnation? When God calleth you to a
rekening, what cá you haue to answere?
Are ye any better then the Gergezites,
which desiered Christe to departe from
them because they loste their hogges
and swyne? yea, ye are worse then they
were by muche, because ye haue profes
sed Christe ád receaued him and his doctrine, and with him vnspeakable bene-
fytes and treasors. And yet notwithstan
ding haue not onely desiered him to departe from amongest you as they did:
but layde violent handes vpon him, per
secuting him with sword, banishmét, fire, and cruell death, as thogh he had bene your mortal enimy. O ingratitude
intolerable! Christe your mercifull Lor
de (who destroyed nothinge of yours,
but preserued and increased, euen your

Worldely cómodities preferred to spiritual benefites

Mat 9.

m.

ſwine & hogges, & all other beaſtes ãd cattell in great abudance) you haue deſpiced and vtterly denied, to haue Antichriſte to be your Lorde ãd gouernour, ãd with hĩ all filthie ſwine, wilde beares, wolues, bores, tygers, and lyons to deuoure, deſtroye, ãd ouerthrowe all thinges: not your fieldes ãd paſtures onely: but villages, Townes, Cities, and Caſtels, yea your ſelues, your wyues, and children, and what ſo euer you counte moſte precious.

Wel, the day of the Lorde will come, when you ſhal fele what it is to fight for your Maſſe, and to betraye the Goſpell, to riſe and rebell agaynſte your lawfull Prĩce, ãd to obeye ãd defende a baſtarde, and opẽ enimie to God, an vtter deſtruction of the whole realme: to murther and baniſhe your naturall countriemẽ ãd louing brethern, to honor ãd receaue ſtrangers Gods expreſſe aduerſaries: a cruell people, a prowde nation: a people of a farre and of a ſtrange langage, whoſe tõgue ye ſhall not vnderſtãde, an impudẽt natiõ, ãd hard harted people, with out all pitie and mercie, which nether will be moued with the lamẽtable voyce of the mothers, nor ſhewe

Baruch. 4
Ieremi. 5.
Deut. 28.

anie compaſsion for the pittifull crye
of their ſucklinges and infantes. And
whiſbecauſe ye haue choſé to obeye vile man, yea a raginge and madé womá,
rather then the almightie and mercifull
God.Repent,repent, ô ye people of England, for your deſtruction is at hande.
Forſake with ſpede the vnlawfull obediéce of fleſhe and bloude,ád learne to ge
ue honor í tyme to the liuíg Lorde,that
he maye ſtaye his háde,ád drawe to him
agayne his ſtretched out arme,that you
may ſynde mercie,and that the bothom
of your cupp be not turned vpwarde.

A Godly
and moſte
neceſſarie
admonitió

Alas ſaye you,what is this we heare?
Be not the people, of them ſelues as ſhe
epe without a paſtor?If the Magiſtrates
and other officiers cótemne their duetie
in defending Gods glorie and the Lawes
cómitted to their charge, lieth it in our
power to remedie it? Shall we that are
ſubiectes take the ſworde in our hádes?
It is in dede as you ſay,a great diſcoura
ging to the people whé they are not ſtir
red vp to godlyneſſeby the good exáple
of all ſortes of Superiors, Magiſtrates
ád officers in the faithefull executíg of
their office:ád ſo muche more whé they

The vaine
excuſes of
the people.

m ii.

are not defended by them in their right
and title, as wel concerning religion, as
the freedome of their naturall coūtrie:
but moste of all when they, which shuld
be ther guydes ād Capitayns, are become instrumétes to inforce them to wicked impietie. Neuertheles, all this can
be no excuse for you, seing, that euil
doinges of others, whether they be Lor
des, Dukes, Barōs, knights or any inferior officers, may not excuse you in e-
uil. And thoghe you had no man of
power vpon your parte: yet, it is a sufficient assurance for you, to haue the
warrāt of Godds worde vpon your side,
and God him self to be your Capitayne
who willeth not onely the Magistrates
ād officers to roote out euil from amon
gest them, beit, idolatrie, blasphemie or
open iniurie, but the whole multitude
are therwith charged also, to whō a portiō of the sworde of iustice is cōmitted,
to execute the iudgementes which the
Magistrates lawfully commande. And
therfore if the Magistrates would whollye despice and betraye the iustice and
Lawes of God, you which are subiectes
with them shall be condemned except
you

Deu. 4. 5
& 6.
1. Chro.
29.

you mayntayne and defend the same
Lawes agaynst them, ād all others to the
vttermoste of your powers, that is, with
all your strēgth, with all your harte and
with all your soule, for this hath God
required of you, ād this haue you promi
sed vnto him not vnder cōdition (if the
Rulers will) but without all exceptiōs to
do what so euer your Lorde and God
shall commande you.

Exod. 17

As touching idolatrie, it is worthie
to be considered what Moyses wryte-
the, or rather the Spirite of God by hī,
how the Lorde in that place chargeth
the whole people to stone to death with
out mercy the false Prophet or drea-
mer, when anie shulde rise vp amongest
thē, yea thoghe the thinges came to pas
se which he before spake, if that therby
he soght to perswade thē or drawe thē to
idolatrie. And also howe he suffred such
amōgest his people to try ād proue thē,
whether they woulde loue him with all
their harte and with all their soule, mea
nīg (as euery mā may well perceaue) that
if they shulde yelde for all their signes
ād wonders to idolatrie, ād not punishe
such false Prophetes and dreamers as

Deut. 13.

m, iii.

God had raysed vp: that thē that they loued
him not, yea that they had playnly forsaken and denied him, for that he commanded expreslye that euerie such Prophet shuld be put to death, and therfore
chargeth to take the euill frō amongest
them. Which commandemēt as it is not
geuen onely to the Rulers and Gouernours (thoghe I confesse it chieflie apperteyneth to their office to see it execu
ted, for which cause they are made Rulers) but also is comon to all the people,
who are likewise bownde to the obser-
uation of the same: euenso is the punish
ment appoynted of God, belonging to
all maner of persons without exception,
being found transgressors. For the Lorde is a iust punisher, with whom there is
Ecclesi. 35
Deut. 10.
Leui. 19.
no respecte of persons, who willeth his
people to be like him in their iudgemē-
tes. In iudgemēte (saithe the Lorde) co-
mitte no vnrighteousnes, nether respect
the face of the poore, nether be you a-
frayde at the cōtenaūce of the mightie,
but iudge vprightly to your neghbour.
Deut. 13.
    Moreouer that euery persone both
high and lowe is charged of God with
this Lawe, and none freede from the pu-
nishmēt, it is euidēt in the same Chapter

folowing: Where God doth not permit somuche as priuie whispering in thy eare, tending to idolatrie, vnpunished, no not of thy dearest frende or kinsmā, sayng: Yf thine owne naturall brother, sonne, daughter, or the wyffe of thine owne bosome, or thy neghboure whom thou loueste as thine owne liffe, secreatly prouoke thee to idolatrie, to serue strāge Gods, either farre or neare, geue not place to him, nether heare him, nether let thine eye haue pitie vpō hī, nether shalt thou pardō him, or hide him, but shalt vtterly sley hī: thy hande shall first be vpon such a one to kill him, and then the handes of all the people &c. *what zeale we oght to God in punishinge idolatrers.*

The like commandement is also geuen in the 17. and 18. Chap. of the same boke, charging all the people of God in generall, to see idolatrie punished without mercie, and that in all persones. Wherfore we may moste certaynely conclude, that if the Rulers and Magistrates in this case, woulde not execute the Lawes of God where with they are so straightly charged, that then the people are not discharged, excepte they put it in execution to take

the euil from amongeſt them, to whom
it alſo belongeth. Next, that no perſone
is exempted by any Lawe of God from
this puniſhment, be he kinge, Quene or
Emperour, that is, either openly or pri-
uely knowne to be an idolatrer be he
neuer ſo neare or deare vnto vs, he muſt
dye the death. For God hath not placed
them aboue others to tranſgreſſe his
Lawes as they liſte, but to be ſubiecte
vnto them as well as others, ouer whom
they gouerne. And if they be ſubiecte
vnto his Lawes, they muſte be ſubiect to
the puniſhment alſo, when they be
fownd diſobedient tranſgreſſors: yea, ſo
muche the more as their example is mo
re daungerous. For looke what wicked-
neſſe reigneth in the Magiſtrates, the
ſubiectes comonly take incouragement
therby to imitate the ſame, as we ſee in
the examples of Ieroboam. Achab and
wicked Manaſſes, who being ſuffred in
the beginninge to commit idolatrie,
and to erecte idoles, made the ſame likewiſe laufull to all their ſubiectes. For
the ſame cauſe God commãded Moyſes
to hãge vp all the capitaynes and heads
of the people, for that by their example
they made the people idolatrers alſo: he

As al perſones oght to obey Godes Lawes, ſo oght they to be puniſhed if they tranſgreſſe them.

1. king.
14.21.

Num. 25.

had no respect to their auctoritie, be
cause they were Rulers, but so muche
the rather woulde he haue them so sharp-
lie punished, that is, hanged agaynst
the sunne without mercy: which iudgement, thoghe it was done at Gods com-
mandiment firste, and after at Moyses,
yet were the people executors of the
same, and all did vnderstand that it was
iuste : and not for that tyme onely, but
to be a perpetuall example for euer, ād
a sure admonition of their duetie in the
like defectiō from God, to hāge vp such
Rulers as shulde drawe them frō him.

And thoghe it appeare at the firste
sight a great disordre, that the people
shulde take vnto them the punishment
of transgression, yet, when the Magistrates and other officers cease to do
their duetie, they are as it were, without officers, yea, worse then if they had
none at all, and then God geueth the
sworde in to the peop'es hande, and he
him self is become immedialty their head (Yf they will seeke the accomplish-
ment of his Lawes) and hath promised
to defende them and blesse them. *Leui.26:*

And althogh the rebellion of the *Deu 27.30*

people, their ingratitude and contempte of Godes Lawes hath bene such at all tymes, that it is a rare thinge to ſhewe their duetie in this behalf, by anye exáple: yet is there one facte of the Iſralites worthie memorie, ád appertaynig, to this purpoſe, whiche is written in the boke of the Iudges, at what tyme they had no lawfull Magiſtrate in all Iſraell. Who notwithſtandinge roſe vp whollie together agaynſt the Tribe of Beniami in Gabaa (becauſe of that ſhamefull vilanie, which the ſonnes of Belial had done to the Leuites wiffe) and ſayed or agreed amongeſt them ſelues, that none ſhuld departe to their houſes or tentes, before they were reuenged of their owne brethern the Beniamites, to ſlea thoſe deteſtable perſons, which had ſo ſhamefully abuſed the Leuites wiffe, albeit ſhe was an harlot, and they without a guide or Capitayne: not knowing when they came to the felde who ſhulde be their gouernour to leade thé, and geue the onſet, before they had cóſulted with God, who appoynted vnto them Iuda. Here do we ſee the eleuen

Ind. 19. 20

The cómó people wtth out a Gouernour prepare shé ſelues to warre.

Tribes

Tribes, to whome the Leuite made his complaynt, in sendinge to euery Tribe a portion of his wiffe , did not excuse them selues to shew iustice , bicause they wanted a lawfull Magistrate to gouerne them , nor thoght them selues discharged for that they were as sheeppe without a pastor : except they did thus arme them selues againste the sonnes of Belial the vngodly Beniamites to see the Iudgementes ofGod executed accordinge to hisLaw(and as they saide them selues)to cut of the euil frō amon gest,then demādinge in the end the wic ked mē that had cōmitted that vilanie.

But you wil say:It is an other matter for the people to enterprice such an acte being without a Ruler , and when they haue a Ruler appoynted vnto them , without whom they may do nothing.To this I answered before,that it is all one to be without a Ruler,and to haue such as will not rule in Gods feare . Yea it is much better to be destitut altogether , then to haue a tyrant and murtherer . For then are they nomore publik persons , contemning their pu-

blik auctoritie in vſinge it agaynſt the
Lawes, but are to be taken of all men,
as priuate perſones, and ſo examyned
and puniſhed.Neuer the leſſe,to the intent ye may vnderſtande, that the gouernour oght not to take away all right from the people,nether diſcharge thē
vtterly, from the execution of iuſtice:
let vs conſider a like example of the
peoples zele vnder the worthie Capitayne Ioſua,who when they but harde
that the Sonnes of Ruben, the Sonnes of
Gad, and the half Tribe of Manaſſes,
had erected vp an Altar in their portiō,
which God had geuen them beyonde
Iordane, thinking that they had ſo done, to haue ſacrificed theron, and ſo to
haue fallen from God: aſſembled them
ſelues together wholly,agaynſt the Ru
benytes,Gaddites and half Tribe of Ma
naſſes to reuenge their defection from
God(as they tooke it)thoghe afterwarde they proued it to be nothing ſo.
Which facte, as it declared an earneſt
true zele in the people for the defence of Gods glorye, and his religion : ſo
Ioſua their Capitayne, nether did nor
ought

Ioſua.22.

The people
aſſemble in
Gods cauſe.

OR DISOBEY. 189

ought to haue reproued them: yea,
happie might Iosua thinke him self,
that had his people so readie to mayntayne of their owne accorde the Lawes of God, whiche before in the dayes
of Moyses were so stubburne and rebellious. And if this redinesse was com
mendable, hauing a worthie Magistrat
and godly Capitayne: how necessary is
it to be vsed amongest the people when
they haue vngodly and wicked Princes, who seke by all means to drawe
them rather from the Lawe of God,
then to incourage them to mayntayne
the same? Wherfore this zele to defend Gods Lawes and preceptes, wherewith all sortes of men are charged, it
is not onely prayse worthie in all, but
requyred of all, not onely in abstayninge
ge from the transgression of the sayed
Lawes, but to see the iudgemétes therof
executed vpon all maner of persones
with out exception. And that if it be not
done by the consent and ayed of the
Superiours, it is lawfull for the people,
yea it is their duetie to do it thé selues,
as well vpon their owne rulers and Ma-

giſtrat, as vpon other of their bretherē, hauing the worde of God for their warrant, to which all are ſubiecte, and by the ſame charged to caſt forthe all euill from them, and to cut of euery rotten membre, for feare of infecting the whole body, how deare or pretious ſo euer it be. If death be deſerued, death: if other puniſhmétes, to ſee they be executed in all.

Rom. 13.

For this cauſe haue you promiſed obedience to your Superiors, that they might herein helpe you: and for the ſame intent haue they taken it vpon them. If they will ſo do, and keepe promiſſe with you accordinge to their office, then do you owe vnto them all humble obedience: If not, you are diſcharged, and no obedience belongeth to them: becauſe they are not obedient to God, nor be his miniſters to puniſhe the euell, and to defend the good. And therfore your ſtudie in this caſe, oght to be, to ſeeke how you may diſpoſe and puniſhe according to the Lawes, ſuch rebells agaynſt God, and oppreſſers of your ſelues and your countrie: and not how to pleaſe them, obeye

them,

them , and flatter them as you do in their impietie. Which is not the waye to obtayne peace , and quietneſſe , but to fall in to the handes of the allmightie God , and to be ſubiecte to his fearefull plagues and puniſhmentes.

CHAP. XIIII.

This is no doctrine of Rebellion, but the onely doctrine of peace and means to inioye quietlie the comfortable bleſſinges of God, which oght not to be wiſſhed for onely of the people , but carefully ſoght for alſo.

Nd althoghe this ſeeme a ſtrange doctrine, perrelous, and to moue ſedition amõgeſt the peo ple , and to take from the lawfull Rulers all due obedience: yet whoſo will conſider the matter a right, ſhall finde it ſou nde and true doctrine , and the onely doctrine of godly peace and quietneſſe, and means to auoyde all ſtrief and rebellion, by whiche onely Superiors ſhall rule in the feare of God,

and subiectes reuerently obeye them
without grudging or murmuring. For is
there anie lawes more parfit then are
the Lawes of God? Or did anie mā better
know the nature of man, then he which
created man? Or anie more desierous to
keepe them in his feare, and true obedy
ence, then God him self, who chose them
for his people? Then who is so mad and
Godwhich impudēt, to thinke that peace ād quiet-
made man nesse can be amongest anie people or
knoweth nation, by obseruing the Lawes of wic-
beʃt what ked men, rather then in reteyning the
Lawes are wholsome Lawes of God? That mā whi-
moʃte expe ch is not able to rule him selfe, can bet-
dient for ter gouerne his subiectes and defende
his preʃer- them, than God may his people? That
uation. the people shall rather enioye all blessinges of God, in yelding to the wickednesse of the vngodlie Rulers, then to see
them straightlie punished for transgressions of the confortable Lawes of the almightie? For after that God had once ge
uen his Lawes to his people, he shewed
them playnlie by Moyses that he requi-
Deut. 10. red nothing els of them, but to feare
him and to walke in his wayes, to loue
him, and serue him with all their harte
and

and to keepe his preceptes and statutes,
which he commanded them that day. And
why? bycause (saithe Moyses) he is the
God of Gods, the Lorde of Lordes, the
greate mightie and dreadful God, whiche hath no respecte of persones, nor taketh anie rewardes.   And this fructe
shall you be suer of in keepinge his Lawes. He wilbe your prayse, ad your God: *Deut. 4.*
that is (as in an other place the same
Moyses writeth) He will make you a wise
people, a mightie Nation, praysed and
commeded of all Natios, which shall saye,
This is onlie a wise people, and a people
of vnderstandinge ad mightie. For what
people is so great, whiche hath their God
so friendly and familiar with them, as
the Lorde our God is in all thinges that
we call to him for? For whiles we obey
his Lawes, and suffer them in no case, ad
in no persone to be transgressed and left
vnpunished (to the vttermoste of our po
wer) we are assured that the blessinges
which God after promised, shalbe pow-
red vpo vs: that is to be blessed at home *Deut. 28.*
and a brode, in the frute of our wombe,
of our lande, of our beastes and cattell.
And the Lorde will make our enemies

which rife agaynft vs to fall before vs,
to entre in one waye agaynft vs, and to
flee by feuen wayes afore vs. And all
the people of the earthe fhall fee that
the Name of the Lorde is called vpon
amongeft vs, and fhall be afrayde of
vs.

Yt is then no newe doctrine which
God fo longe ago taught to the Ifraelites, nor no rafhe or perelous doctrine
wherby they are onely made wife, and
mofte ftrongly defended. Nether yet
dothe it minifter occafion of rebellion,
without which there can be no godlie
peace or quietneffe, as your experience
in Englande hath all readie (as I fuppo-
fe) fufficiently taught you : who haue
felt rather hellike tormentes, and fhamefull confufion, fince ye permitted
the wilde bores to cafte downe the
hedge of the Lordes vinyarde, that is,
his Lawes and preceptes, then anie maner of godly peace, either in confciences or bodies: which miferie fhall haue
no end before you reclayme with a ve-
hement zele and loue, your right title
and poffeffion of Gods Lawes, which
you

Let your owne confcieces be Iudges in this behalfe

you haue moſte vnthankfully geuen
ouer and neglected.

Yf the true zele of Gods people had
bene in you when poperie began to be
preached in the place of the Goſpell,
when the Maſſe was reduced in place of
the Lordes ſupper, and that by the ignorant Papiſts and malicious ſhaue-
lyngs, when Antichriſt was reſtored to
diſplace Chriſt: coulde ye haue ſuf-
fered this vnponiſhed? Or if you had pu
niſhed it as you were then charged by
Gods Lawes and mans, durſte they haue proceaded to ſuch impietie? If you
had required the Magiſtrates to rule
you in Gods feare and not in tyrannie,
and that you woulde reuerence them as
Gods miniſters ſo rulinge you, otherwiſe, not to acknowledg them but as
his enimies, and ſo to take them: durſt
either that Ieſabel ſo ragingly haue
trodé Gods worde the Goſpell of Chriſt
our Sauiour as a polluted ſowe vnder
her feete, either els ſo raſhely deſtroy-
de her fathers and brothers Lawes before her? Durſte ſhe without all ſhame ſo openly and vnfaythfully haue
broken promiſſe to them (whiche

The con-
tempt of
Gods wo-
rde is the
dore to all
licentious
wicked-
nes.

to their owne sorrow, and all others this
day) were her chief promoters? Assure
your selfs no. If you had required all
Massemongers, and false Preachers to
haue bene punished with deathe (as is
appoynted by Gods worde for such bla
sphemers and idolatrers, and if they to
whom it apperteyned, had denyed, your
selues would haue seen it performed at
all tymes, and in all places) then shuld
you haue shewed that zele of God, whi-

Num. 25. ch was cōmended in Phinees, destroyinge the adulterers: and in the Israelites
againste the Ber iamites, as before is no
ted. Ye then had not the Pristes of Baal
so swarmed abrode, nor the seruātes of
God haue bene in such abundāce murthered. But great was our synnes before, that this deserued: and colde was our
zele to Godwardes after, that this shame haue suffred: and grosse is our blynd
dulnes, whiche wil not yet see nor seeke
to remedie it.

what ru-
les are to
be obsrrued
in resisting
the superi-
or powers
 Neuerthelesse in all these enterprises
you muste be certaine and sure of this
one thinge, that vnder the name of Religion and pretence to promote Gods
glorie, you seeke not either your priuate

te gaynes or promotiõ, as did all the car
nall Gofpelers, and fuch as would be cõ
ted the chief pillers and mainteyners of
the fame in tymes paft amongeft you.
And therfore vnder the cloke of Chrift,
feekyng the worlde, when Chrift fe-
med to haue the vpper hande : are now
returned to their oldemaifter Antichrifte, to be his hired fouldiars, and to fight
vnder his banner agaynft Chrift and
his feruantes, by whom they were firfte
promoted. Which treafon God is prepared all redie to reuenge, to pluck from
them his fethers, and to fet furth to the
whole worlde their fhame and naked-
neffe. For he is a iuft God, and hateth Pfal.5.
iniquitie, and therfore will be no cloke
to couer their falfhode and couetouf-
neffe.

Alfo ye muft beware that priuate
difpleafure, and worldly iniuries moue
you not more to feeke reuengement of
your aduerfaries, then the true zele and
thirfte of Gods worde, the liuely foode
of your foules. For then do you feeke
your felues, and not God: then take you
his office out of his hande, to whom ye
oght to commit all your private dif-

Deu 32.
Exoch. 9
Rom. 12.

pleasures and iniuries : then can ye not
loke to haue Gods right hande vpon
your parte, but rather may be assured
to finde him your enimie, and strongly
armed against you. To resiste euill therfore is your parte, and to mayntayne
Godlynesse, but symply and vnfaynedly, for the loue of vertue, and hatred
of vice, yf you will be sure to prosper,

Psal. 7.
Iere. 17.

and auoyde Gods heauy displeasure,
who is the sercher of your hartes and
secreats, and will in tyme disclose
them and make them knowen to all
men.

   But you perchaunce would graunt me all this, that it is both lawfull
and godly, if the people wholie to gether woulde follow the example of ze-

A doute
which tro
bleth the
people.

lous Phinees and the Israelites, as before was mentioned, and take punishment them selues vpon all blasphemers of God, manifest betrayers of
their countrie, and cruell murtherers
of their brethern : seing the Lawes of
God and publycke peace can be by
no other means restored. But when
the people them selues agree not,

when

when they are deuided amongeſt them
ſelues, and the greateſt parte of them
perchance papiſtes, and will be maynteyners of ſuch vngodly proceadings
as are now broght in to Englande,
how is it poſsible that by the weaker
parte, Gods glory ſhulde be reſtored?

    To this I anſwere, that as I know
the reſtoringe of Gods worde, and *The anſ-*
comfortable doctrine of our Sauiour *were.*
Chriſte to be the onely worke of
God, and of no man (thoghe he forſake not man as a meane external)
and alſo am not ignorant that he re-
gardeth not the multitude and ſtren-
ghe of man to accompliſhe his purpoſe, who hath bene accuſtomed to *Num. 13.*
geue the victorie to a few in nom- *1 Sam. 14.*
ber, and weake in ſtrengh, that the *Iudith 9.*
glorie might be his: ſo will I not *Iudges 6.*
counſelle you raſhely to caſt your
ſelues in to danger, but patiently and
erneſtly to call to the lyuing Lorde for
mercy, and acknowledging your ſynnes (for which this plague is powred v-
pon you) to deſier him to ſhewe ſome ſi-

n. iiii.

gne of conforte : who hath promiſed to
heare your groninges, and to beholde
your affliction, as he did the groninges

Exod. 2.3   and oppreſſion of his people in Egypt,
when they were broght to full repen-
tance ād ſealing of their ſynnes: ſo that
he came downe from heauen, ād appeared to Moyſes , and ſent him to be their
Capitayne, whom they once had forſa-
ken: as you haue done Chriſte.

Iudg .3.   And as he alſo ſent Othoniel to deliuer his people, whē they cryed vntohim
in that captiuitie that they were in vn-

A ſuer ſig-   der the idolatrous kynge of Meſopo-
ne that   tamia for the ſpace of eight yeres.
God hear-
eth our pra   Nether is this ynough to call vpon
yer when   God for helpe, except ye vtterly forſa-
he geuith   ke the wicked doctrine and doinges of
vs a mea-   the papiſtes, ād ſeeke alſo (to the vtter-
ne to deli-   moſt of your power) for remedie in fo-
uer vs.   lowing the example of the people of
God, as it is writen : whiche did not o-
nely ſerue God and call to him for helpe, at what tyme they were deſtitute of

1. Mach.6   their worthie Capitayne Iudas Macha-
beus: but alſo ſoght it, and demanded it
where it was like to be founde. And aſ-

semblinge them selues together, came to Ionathan his brother, desiering him to be their guide and Capitayne, to helpe them in their miserie, and to defende them agaynst the enimies of God, their whole nation being then moste cruelly oppressed on euery side, and the moste parte of them in vile slauery, seruinge the strage Gods of the heathen. The Ionatha pityinge their estate and his owne, did not deny their requeste, but willingly toke in hande that dangerous enterprise, beige assured that the cause was lawfull, to maintaine to his power Gods glorie ad to succour his afflicted natio, as his brother Iudas had done before him. And doinge the same with a simple eye, accordinge as he was boude, God prospered his doinge, and he had good successe

Therfore yf they did well in demadinge succour, and he discharged his conscience in graunting their request, why is it not also lawfull for you to seeke helpe of the that be able ad willing: and for them likewise to graute helpe, to whom God hath lente it for that vse especially?

But I know your answere: experience (saye you) hath taught vs the contrary. For if God had bene pleased herein withe Syr Thomas Wyat that valiant Capitayne taking in hande the like enterprise: it shulde vndoutedly haue had better successe. But he being a man, and of God, of great estimation amongest all goodmen, was notwithstandinge apprehended, condemned, and at the last (althogh he was promised his pardon) as a traytor beheaded. And besides him Sir Henry Isley knight, with many godely men for the same facte, hanged, and murthered. The like also ye will affirme of that Noble man Henry Lorde Graye, Marques Dorset, ád Duke of Suffolke: who onely for the zeale that he had to promote Gods glorie, and the libertie of his countrie, prepared him self with that power he coulde make to the ayde of the sayed Wyat, according to his promisse. But beinge deceaued, or rather betrayed by such as he trusted vnto, was in the ende also apprehended, and with his brother the Lorde Thomas Gray (a Gentleman of great courage, and

Sir Henry Isley.

The Duke of Suffolk

The Lorde Thomas Graye.

and towardnesse, likewise beheaded.

Althogh I minde not to stand long in the praise of these worthye més factes, who moste cowardly were of many betrayed, which since perchance haue felt some parte of worse misery: yet so muche must I nedes confesse in their behalf, that none but papistes, or traytors can iustly accuse them of treason or disobedience. Of whó to be misdained or slandered, is in the eyes of the godly, no small cómendation, ád prayse. For to passe ouer with siléce the duke of Sulffolke (whose noble parétage and ernest loue that he bare to the promoting of Christes Gospell, and the welth of his coútrie, is to all Englishe men sufficiently knowne) what I beseche you moued Wyat that worthy knight to rise? Was it his pouertie? Beholde, he was a famous Gétleman of great landes and possessions, stowt and liberall in the seruice of his Prince, faithefull to his countrie, and mercifull to the poore. Soght he ambitiously honour? Which of his enemies coulde herewith iustly charge him? Did he this bicause he was of a troublesome ád busy nature, which

coulde not be vnder lawfull gouernement. His great wisedome, modestie, ād
gentle behauiour at all tymes, ād to all
persons, did well declare the contrary: euer more being founde a faythfull
Capitayne to his Prīce in the fielde, ād
an obediét subiecte at home. What thē
moued him to this dangerous entreprise? Verely, the zeale of Gods trueth
and the pitie that he had to his Countrie, for the miseries he sawe to appro-

what mo-
ued M. wy
t t to this
enterprise.

che by the vsurped power of vngodly
Iesabell, and her merciles papistes the
sowldiars of Antichriste. Yf it be treasō
to defend the Gospel and his Countrie
frome cruel strangers and enemies, thē
was Wyat a traytor ād rebell. but if this
was his duetye, and all others that professed Christe amōgest you, then are all
such traytours, as did deceaue him: and
such as toke not his parte also, whē tyme ād occasiō by him was iustly offered.

And thogh his enterprise had not
such sucesse, as we would haue wisshed:
yet was it no worse then our cowardnes
se, and vnworthinesse deserued. Whiche
nether oght of anie therfor to be condemned, nether shulde be anie discoura
gement

gemét to others in the like. For some ty
mes we see the verie seruantes of God to
haue euill successe in their doinges, according to más iudgement: and yet God
is well pleased therwith. As the example
of the Israelites, wherof we made mention before dothe moste manifestlie ap
proue: at what tyme they armed them
selues agaynst the Beniamites, and that
at the commandement of God, and yet
were twise disconcfyted, losing the first
tyme 22. thousand men: and the next
day folowing 18.thowsand:bothetymes,
consulting with the Lorde, and folowing
his commandement.

How dan
gerous it is
to iudge
the cause
by the successe.
Iud.29

If thou wilt here pronounce accordíg to the effecte, behold, thou shalt pre
ferre the vile ád adulterous Beniamites
to the seruaútes of God: those which mo
ste abhominably abused the Leuites
wiffe, to them that with the zele of God
soght to haue the transgression punished. Euen so, saye I of worthie Wyat. Yf
you iudge his facte accordíng to the suc
cesse in mans reason: then shall you pre
farre to him all the false and flattering
Counsellers, all wicked and blouddy
Bishoppes, and all others that would be

counted Nobles, which in very dede be
traytours to God and his people. But
Wyat, I dowte not, departed with prayse
the seruant of God, where all thefe are
left to perpetual ſhame and deſtruction
without ſpeedie repentance. O noble
Wyat, thou art now with God, and
thoſe worthy men that died for that en-
terpriſe! Happy art thou, and they which are placed in your euerlaſtinge inhe-
ritance, and freed from the miſerie of ſu
che as were your enimics, in ſo iuſte and
lawfull a cauſe: who liue as yet patrones
of idolatrers, of theues and murtherers,
agaynſt whō thou and thine ſhall ſtande
one daye as iudges to their cōdénation.

For what can you Nobles or Coūſel-
lers ſaye for your ſelues at that daye, whē
God ſhall call you to accompt (ye knowe not how ſone) which haue permitted
Wyat, and with him the whole Churche
and comon welth of England to fall into the handes of Gods enimies, and
would not reſkewe him, ſome of you
hauing then in your handes ſufficient
power not onely to haue ſupported him
and others which ſeare God accordinge
to duety ād promiſſe: but to haue tamed
                                   the

the ráping lyons, raginge beares, ãd ra-
ueninge wolues? Haue ye not herein iuftly códemned your felues as faynt harted cowardes and manifefte trayters,
not onely to Wyat, but to God him felf,
to his poore oppreffed feruantes, and to
your owne natiue and ruyñous coũtrie?
But your vngodly fetches and wicked
doinges (wherof I am not all together i-
gnorant) with your names, I do now pur
poflye omitte: perchãce God in the mea
ne feafon will chaunge your myndes,
fofté your harde hartes, and call you to
repentáce. Otherwife doute ye nothíge,
but God will minifter either to me, or
fome other(or it belonge)the like occafion to fet forth your fhame and naked-
neffe to all pofteritie, as you mofte worthely haue deferued: who hithervnto ha
ue fhewed your felues (in contemnyng
fo many ãd notable occafiós offered by
Gods prouidence, as well fynce as in the
dayes of Wyat)to be mé in whom is ne
ther zele to religion, nor loue to your
coũtrie. And therfore I leauinge you to
Gods mercies, or fearefull iudgementes,
will fpeake a worde or two by the waye.
to thé which will be calledGofpellers, ãd

The condẽ nation of the Nobles in for- fakinge Wyat.

Gofpellers fearinge man more then God are made inftrumẽts of Satan.

yet haue armed them selues agaynst the
Gospel drawing forth with them out of
their countrie to mayntayne Philipps
warres, and to please Iesabel (who seeketh by that means, to cut their throtes
craftely) their poore and ignorant tena-
tes and other souldiars without knowledge, whiles their brethern be burned
at home and their countrie like to be wa-
sted, spoyled, oppressed, possessed, and re
plenished with vngodly Spanyardes. Is
this the loue that ye beare to the worde
of God? (ô ye Gospellers) haue ye bene
so taught in the Gospel to be wilfull
murtherers of your selues, and others a-
brode, rather then lawfull defenders of
Gods people, and your countrie at home? Is Gods cause become iniuste ad not
meete to be defended: and the cruel mur
ther and shamefull slaughter of Princes
approued? This hathe not the Gospell
taught you, but chieflye in all your
doinges to seeke the kingdome of God,
next to loue your neighbour as your sel
ues: and in no case to be murtherers (as
all you are) that either for pleasure of
Princes, or hope of promotion, or gayne
of wages are become Capitayns, or soul
diars,

diars in vnlawfull warres, especially in
this cafe and daungerous tyme.

Then which of you all now for fhame
can accufe that zelous and godly man
Wyat, whither ye be of the Nobles,
Coûfellers, Lords, knightes, or of the co
mon fouldiars? I wil make your owne
confciences iudges in this matter, whither worthie Wyat or you fhuld be takē
for traytors? He, who in the feare of God
and loue towardes his countrie foght to
defende all, ãd to diftroye none: or you,
who feekinge the deféce of none, labour
to deftroy all? He, who indeuered him
felf to withftande wicked Iefabel, and
the onely traytors of Gods truthe, and
their coûtrie, as Priefts, Bifhopps, and pa
piftes: or you that haue bene their mayn
teyners, with fhildes ãd bucklers. He, w-
ho according to the worde of God, foght
with the daunger of all his goods, landes, and liffe, to keepe out ftrãgers, which were comynge to rule ouer you, and
to deuoure you: or you, which haue bene meanes with your liues, lands, and
goodes to bringe them in, and to defend
them? He, who would be openly knowen
in his doinges as he was in harte, their e-

*whither
wyat and
thofe that
died with
him: or the
Counfele-
rs Nobles
and other
that yet
lyue are
traytours.*

e.

ni̇mie:or you which hate them inwardly, and yet do what you may to shewe your selues friendes outwardly? But tell me your gaynes in the end. To conclude, he who did his indeuour amonge his contriemen at home to defend them, or you whiche helpinge your enemies abrode, labour to destroie your friédes and countrie at home?

Souldiars goinge wi̇th their Captayns to vnlawfall warres and leuing their coũry destitute, are rebells to God and traytours to their country. Gen. 9. Deut. 5. Leui. 24. The condē nation of London in forsakinge Wyat.

Also you subiectes ád souldiars, which are gone with them to butcher your selues and others without cause or cóscience, contrarie to the worde of God, be you assured that before him you shall be con demned as rebells and disobedient persones, where as your godly bretheren which in a iust and lawfull cause died with faithfull Wyat, are alowed before God, and of all goodmen commended.

O London, London, thou that boasted thy self to be the Ierusalem of all Englá de, wherin Christ chieflie was preached, and the truethe of his Gospell best knowne, reméber how thou forsookest that godly Capitayne, ád what promisse thou madest him. Thou (I say) which mightest haue bene an example and cóforte to all the Cities, and Townes in Englande, ád

to

to haue made the papiſtes to tremble ãd
quake for feare . God graunt that for
thy faynt harte in that behalf, and ſhamefull falling from God in murthering
then and ſynce ſo many of his ſeruantes
and Prophetes, thou be not left likewiſe
deſtitute and deſolate, not one ſtone left
vpon a nother, as happened to Ieruſalẽ. Mat.24.
Thou canſt not herein defende thy ſelf,
which ſynce haſt bene readie,and yet art
to maintayne wicked Ieſabell in her tyrannie at home, ãd in her vngodly & ne
deles warres abrode with thy goods and
bodie at her commandement, being ther
by made an ayeder, helper, and furthe-
rer of all her vngodly oppreſſion and ty
rannie. And therfore muſt nedes be par-
taker with her of the dreadfull plagues
and puniſhments , which God hath appoynted for ſuch impietie.

Wherfore to conclude this matter, yſ
Wyats cauſe was iuſte and lawfull, as
thou muſte nedes confeſſe: for if he were fautie in anie poynt,it was chieflie in
this, that he pretended rather the cauſe
of his countrie, then of Gods Religion,
which allwayes oght to be preferred,

and with out the which no Realme or
nation may long cõtynewe in quietnes-
se:for thē God keepeth not watche ouer
thē . Yf alfo he was betrayde of others,
and foght not to betraye any : if he pur-
pofed Gods glorie, and the defence of
his countre : If the iuftnefle of the caufe
oght to trye his doīges, ād not the effect
that folowed, or the preuētíge of tyme,
where vnto he after a forte was inforfed:
thē oght no perfone,whither he be a Ru
ler,or fubiecte, Counfeller, Noble,pu-
blicke or priuate to be difcouraged,but
rather incouraged by Wyats example.
The people to feeke and demandē helpe of thē that are able,and they to graūt
thē fuccour willígly:feeking by all means poffible to reftore Chrift agayne,ād
his kígdome, with whom you haue loft
all godlye libertie ād quietneffe: and to
expell Antichrift and all his adherentes,
by whom you are broght in this miferable flauery and bódage , both of bodies
and foules.

And thoghe it fuccede not the firft or
feconde tyme,no more then did the en-
treprife of Wyat,or of the Ifraelites:yet
when God fhall fee your zele and diligence,

gence, to be applyed onely in seekinge
to maynteyne his kingdome, and the
glorie therof: he wil helpe no dowte at
lenghe to confounde all his enimies, as
he did the thirde tyme confort the Is-
raelits to the vtter destructió of the adulterous Beniamits. We must now looke for no reuelations from the heauens
to teache vs our duety, it being so playnely set before our eyes in his worde.
And if in this case considerately begone
in the feare of God, it shuld happen any
of you to perishe, consider you perishe
but in the fleshe to lyue with God: leauing in the meane tyme an example behinde you, that you liued in his feare
and soght his glorie according to your
duetye.

we oght to be cótented with Gods worde onely and loke for no newe reue lation.

CHAP. XV.

*What remedy or counsell is left, to the poore and af-
flicted seruantes of God, at what tyme they are
destitute of all outwarde meás and supporte of mé.*

TO the people of Israel,
whom God from amon-
ge all nations chose to
be his peculiar people
he did not onely geue
his Lawes, ordinances

and statutes: but also instituted all kinde
of officiers to see the same Lawes put in
execution. And besides this, appoynted
such as might be leaders and defenders
of them in tyme of warre agaynst their
enimes, and such as shuld mayntayne
their right at home in tyme of peace: as
were their iudges and princes appoynted ouer euery Tribe, besides their kinge and chief gouernour, to whome it was
lawfull for the people âu for euery Tribe to resorte in tyme of daunger, to aske counsele and desier helpe, who were
likewise bounde to heare their cause,
and support them, whither it were by
counselle or bodely trauell.

 In like maner God hath no lesse mercifully delte with you in Englande, not
The gra onely geuing vnto you his Lawes and ho
ces of God ly worde, with farre greater light and
towardes playner declaration of his will and plea
Englande sure then euer was published to the Is-
are most a raelits: but also hath furnished you wi-
bundant th all sortes of Magistrates, officers, and
if they wo gouernors necessarie for the accomplish-
uld vse thē hment, or rather execution of the same.
To whom it oght to be no lesse lawfull
      for

for vou to reforte for comforte in your
necefsitie, then it was to the Ifraelites,
and they as muche bownd to heare you.
For this caufe haue you Mayres, Shiriffs,
and Aldermen in Cities, Counftables âd
Bayliffs in Townes, knights âd Iuftices,
in Shires and countries. To thefe oght
the people to haue concurfe in necefsitie, who fhuld be their refuge and ayde
in all trouble and aduerfitie.

But if all thefe be fo fhamfully corrupted, and fo myndles of their charge
and office, that nether the Citezens can
be côforted, nor fuckered by their Mayres, Shiriffes, and Alder men : nether the
poore Townesmen and Tennants by
their Iuftices and Landelordes, but all
geuen ouer as it were to Satan, and to
ferue the luftes of their chief Rulers, care not whether the poore people finke
or fwyme, fo it be well with them (thogh
it be a thinge impofsible that the peo-   *It is impo-*
ple can be diftroyed and they efcape   *fsible for*
daûger, or that their neyghbours houfe   *the people*
câ be confumed with fyer, and theirs re-   *and the*
mayne vntouched) Yf all I faye in whô   *Rulers to*
the people fhuld loke for comforte, wer   *éscape.*

all together declyned from God (as in
dede they apeare to be at this present ty
me in England, without all feare of his
Maiestie or pitie vpon their brethern)
and also, yf the least and weakest parte
of the people in all places feared God,
and all outwarde means of helpe vtterly taken from them, nether being able
to fynde remedie amógest them selues,
nether cã see how to be supported of o-
thers: thé assure your selues (deare brethern and feruants of God) there can be
no better counsell, nor more comfortable or present remedie (which you shall
proue true, if God graunte you his Spirite and grace to folowe it) then in con-
tynual and dayly inuocation of his Name, to rest whollie and only vpon him,
make him your shilde, buckeler and refuge, who hath so promised to be to all
them that are oppressed and depend v-
pon him : to do nothing commanded
agaynst God and your conscience, pre-
ferring at all tymes (as you haue learned before) the will of God, to the will,
punishments, and tyranny of Princes:
sayng, and answeringe to all maner of
per-

perſones: This hath God commanded,
this muſt we do. That hath God forbid-
dé, that will we not do. yf you will robbe vs and ſpoyle vs for doinge the Lordes will, to the Lorde muſt you make
anſwere, and not to vs: for his goodes
they are, and not ours. If ye will impri-
ſone vs, behold, ye are oppreſſors. If ye
will hange vs or burne vs, beholde ye
are murtherers of them which feare the
Lorde, and are created to the Image of
God: for whoſe contempte ye ſhall be
ſtraytly puniſhed. And for our parte, yf
you take from vs this vile and corrup-
tible lyffe, we are aſſured the Lorde
will geue it vs agayne with ioye, and
immortalitie both of bodie and ſoule.

Yf God geue you grace to make
this or the like anſwere, and ſtrength to
contemne their tyrannie, you may be
certayne and ſure to finde vnſpeakable
conforte and quietnes of conſcience,
in the mydle of your danger and greateſt rage of Satan. And thus boldly con-
feſſinge Chriſt your Sauiour before
men (as by the example of thouſande ;
of your bretheren before your faces

God doth mercifully incourage you)
you may with all hope and patience
wayte for the ioyfull confession of
Chrift agayne before his Father and
Angells in heauen, that you are his obe-
diente and dearely beloued seruantes,
being alfo affured of this, that if it be
the will of God to haue you anie longer to remayne in this miserable worlde. that then his prouidence is fo carefull ouer you, ad prefent with you, that
no man or power can take your liffe
from you, nether touche your bodie a-
nie further then your Lorde and God
will permit them. Whiche nether fhall
be augmented for your playne confef-
fion, nor yet diminifhed for keepinge
of filence. For nothing cometh to the
feruants of God by hap or chaúce, whofe heares of their heads are numbred.
Wherof yf you be fo affured as you
oght to be, there can be nothing that
fhuld make you to fhrinke from the Lor
de. If they do caft you in-prifó with Io-
feph, the Lorde will delyuer you: yf they caft you to wilde beafts and lyons, as
they did Daniel, you fhall be preferued:
yf in to the fea with Ionas, ye fhall not
be

Tyrantes can go no further then God permittith.

Mat. 10.

be drowned: or in to the durtie dongeon
with Ieremie, you shall be delyuered: either in to the fyrye furnace withe Sidrach, Misach, and Abednago, yet shall
you not be consumed. Contrarie wise, *None can*
yf it be his good pleasure that you sh- *lose their*
all glorifie his holie Name in your de- *lyfe but by*
ath, what great thing haue you loste? *Godes ap-*
Changing death for liffe, misery for fe- *pointement*
licitie, contynuall vexation and trou-
ble, for perpetuall rest and quietnesse:
chosinge rather to dye with shame of
the worlde being the seruantes of God,
then to lyue amongest men in honor
being the seruantes of Satan, and condemned of God. Otherwise, if you geue place to the wickednesse of men to
escape their malice and bodily dangers,
you shewe your selues therin to feare
man more then the mightie and dreadfull God: him that hath but power of
your bodie, and that at Gods appoyn-
tement, then God him self, who hath po
wer, after he hath destroyed the body,
to cast both bodies and soules in to hell
fyre, there to remayne euerlastingly in
tormentes vnspeakable.

And moreouer that which you loke to obtayne by thefe fhamefull fhi-
efts, you fhall befure to lofe with gryef
and trouble of Confcience. For this fa-
ying of our Maifter being true and certayne, That they which feeke to faue th
eir liffe (meanynge by anie worldly rea
fon or policie) fhall lofe it : what fhall
be their gaynes at lengh, when by dif-
fimulation and yelding to popifhe blafphemie, they difhonor the Maieftie of
God to inioye this fhorte, miferable
and mortall lyffe : to be cafte from the
fauour of God, ãd companie of his heauenly Angells, to inioye for a fhorte tyme their goodes and poffefsions amonge their flefhly and carnall friends:
when as their confcience within fhall
be deeply wounded withe hellike tormentes? when goddes curfe and indignation hangeth contynually ouer the
heades of fuch, ready to be powred downe vpon them? when they fhall finde
no comforte, but vtter difpayer with
Iudas, which for this worldly riches (as
he did) fmade to folde their Maifter: fekinge
either to hange them felues with Iudas, to murther them felues with Fran-
ces

Shamfull
fhifies.

Mat.16.

Of fuch
you haue
had fuffi-
cient profe
before your
eyes.

Iudas.

ces Spera, to drowne them selues with
Iustice Hales, either els to fall in to a ra
ginge madnesse with Iustice Morgen?
What comforte had Iudas then by his
mony receaued for betraynge his Maister? Was he not shortly after compelled to cast it from him with this pitifull
voyce: I haue synned in betraying innocét bloud? Coulde anie of these fore-
named persons, after they had commyt-
ted the like treason to our Sauiour Iesus Christ finde anie more comforte in
their friendes, from whom they were so
loth to departe? Or anie more pleasure
in their possessions, or assurance in their treasures? Beholde, they had all moste miserable lyues for the tyme, and
shamefull endes.

Then deare brethern in Christ,
what other rewarde can anie of you loke for, commytting the like offences?
Haue you anie more assurance of Gods
mercies then they had? Woulde not
Christ spare his owne Apostle Iudas,
and yet will pardon you? Did not iud-
geHales appearingly professe the Gospell a longe space, and was greatly
commended for a godly man amon-

Spera.
Hales.
Morgen

Mat.27.

wicked Day of Chichester was the cause of his desperation gest the Godly? And yet after by the importunate perswations of the pestilent papistes denyinge his Maister, sustayned this horrible iudgment, that he and such like might be a perpetuall example for you and all men to feare the like or worse punishemente.

You see therfore how there is no truste but in God, no comfort but in Christ, no assurance but in his promisse, by whose obedience onely you shall auoyde all danger. And whatsoeuer you lose in this world and suffer for his *Mat.10.* Name, it shall be here recompenced with double according to his promisse, and in the worlde to come with liffe euerlastinge: which is to finde your liffe, when ye are willinge to lay it downe at his commandement.

The second and laste remedie. I am not ignorant how vnnaturall a thinge it is, and contrarie to the fleshe, willingly to sustayne suche cruell deathe, as the aduersaries haue appoynted to all the children of God, myndinge constantly to stand by their profession: which to the spirite notwithstanding is easie and ioyful. For thogh the fleshe be frayle, the spirite is prompte and redy.

Wherof

Wherof (prayſed be the name of God)
you haue had notable experience in ma
ny of your brethern very martyrs of Ch
riſte, who with ioye paciétly and tryum
phinglie, haue ſuffed and drunke with
thurſte of that bitter cupp which nature
ſo muche abhorreth:wonderfully ſtrég-
thned no dowte by the ſecreat inſpira-
tion of Gods holy Spirite. So that there
oght to be none amôgeſt you ſo feeble,
weake or timorous, whom the wonder-
full examples of Godes preſent power
and ſinguler fauour in thoſe perſons,
ſhulde not incourage,bolden,and forti-
fie,to ſhewe the like côſtancie in the ſame cauſe and profeſsion.

    Neuertheles, great cauſe we haue
thankfully to conſider the inſpeakable
mercy of God in Chriſte,which hath far
ther reſpecte to our infirmitie, that w-
hen we haue not that boldeneſſe of ſpi-
rite to ſtande to the death, as we ſee o-
thers, yet geuing ſo muche to our wea-
keneſſe, he hathe prouided a preſent remedie,that beíg perſecuted in one place,
we haue libertie to flee in to a nother:
where we cannot be in our owne coûtrie

with a safe cõsciéce (except we would
make opon profession of our religion,
which is euery mans duetie,and so be
broght to offre vp our liues in sacrifice
to God in testimonie that we are his:)
he hathe mollyfied and prepared the
hartes of stranges to receue vs with all
pitie and gladnesse, where you may be
also not onely delyuered from the feare of death and the papisticall tyrannie
practised without all measure in that
coútrie: but with great freedome of cõscience heare the worde of God contynually preached,and the Sacraments of
our Sauiour Christ purely and duely
ministred,without all dregges of poperie, or supersticion of mans inuention:
to the intent you being with others refresshed for a space, and more strongly
fortified, may be also with others more
re willing and ready to laye downe
your lyues at Gods appoyntment. For
that is the chiefest grace of God, and
greatest perfection,to fight euen to the
bloude vnder Christes banner,and with
him to geue our liues.

But if you will thus flee (welbeloged in the Lord)you must not chose
vnto

vnto your selues places according as
you phantasie, as many of vs which haue left our countrie haue donne : some
dwelling in papisticall places amongest
the enimies of God in the myddle of
impietie : in France, as in Paris, Orliance , and Rone : and some in Italy, as in
Rome, Væenice, and Padua. Which persons in fleeing from their Quene, runne
to the Pope: fearing the daunger of their
bodies , seeke where they may poyson
their soules : thinking by this means to
be lesse suspected of Iesabell , shew
them selues afrayd and ashamed of the
Gospel, which in tymes paste they haue
stowtly professed. And lest they shuld be
thoght fauorers of Christe, haue purpos-
ly ridden by the Churches, and Congre
gations of his seruauntes their bretherne , nether mynded to comforte
others there, nor to be comforted them
selues. Wherin they haue shewed the co
ldenesse of their zele towarde religion,
and geuen no small occasion of slander
to the worde of God, which they seemed
to professe. For beinge returned againe
into their Countrie, they either become
Idolaters with the papistes to please the

Quene, and kepe their poſſeſsions, or
els diſſemblers with the reſt of counter-
fete chriſtians : but to their owne condemnation at length, except the Lorde
graunt vnto them ſpeedie repentance.
For whoſo are aſhamed of Chriſt, and
his Goſpel, thus denying him before mē:
Mat 10. them hath he promiſed to deny, and be
a ſhamed of before his Father, and Angells, in heauen. This maner of fleeinge
then is vngodly, and (as you heare)
daungerous : and therfore not lawfull
for you therin to folow theire example.

Nether is it ynoughe to keepe you
out of the dominions of Antichriſte, ād
to place your ſelues in corners where
you maye be quiete, and at eaſe, and
not burthened withe the chardges
of the poore, thinking it ſufficient if
you haue a litle exerciſe in your houſes in reading a chapiter or two of the
Scriptures, and then wil be counted zelous perſons and great goſpellers. No
brethern and ſiſters, this is not the way
to ſhowe your ſelues manfull ſouldiars
of Chriſt, except you reſorte where his
banner

banner is diſplayed, and his ſtandarde
ſett vppe: where the aſſemble of your
brethren is, and his worde openly preached, and Sacramentes faithfully mini-
ſtred. For otherwiſe, what may a man
iudge, but that ſuch either diſdayne the
compagnie of their poore brethren,
whome they oght by all means to helpe and comfort, according to that
power that God hath geuen them for
that ende onely, and not for their owne
eaſe: or els that they haue not that zele to the houſe of God, the aſſemble of
his ſeruantes, and to the ſpirituall gyftes ãd graces (which God hath promiſed
to powre vpon the diligent hearers of
his worde) as was in Dauid: which deſie-
red being a kinge, rather to be a dore-
keeper in the houſe of God, then to
dwel in the tentes of the vngodlye: la- *Pſal. 4ᵗ*
mentyng nothinge ſo muche the iniu-
ries done vnto him by his ſonne Abſo-
lon (which were not ſmall) as that he
was depryued from the comfortable
exercices in the Tabernacle of the Lorde, which then was in Sion. Nether
dothe there appeare in ſuch per-

Efa.2. fons that greedie defier (wherof Efai ma
keth mention) whiche oght to be in the
profeffers of the Gofpell, who neuer
woulde ceafe or refte, till they fhuld cli-
me vp to the Lordes Hill: meaninge the
Churche of Chrifte, fayng one to a nother: Let vs afcende vp to the Hill of the
Lorde, to the houfe of the God of Iacob, and he will teache vs his wayes, and
we fhall walke in his foote fteppes. For
the Lawe fhall come forthe of Sion, and
the worde of the Lorde from Ierufalem.
Whiche zele the Prophet dothe not me-
tion in vayne, but to fhew what a thurft
and erneft defier fhuld be in the true
Chriftians, and how the fame apeareth
in feekinge and reforrtinge to thofe places, where it is fet forthe in greatefte a-
bundance and perfection, as was after
Chriftes afcention in Ierufalem. And as
that zele fhewed them to be of Chrifte,
by the like muft we be iudged Chriftians alfo, that if we flee for Chrifte,
the places where vnto we flee may
beare witnes for what caufe we are
fledde.

Nether is yt a fufficient excufe
which

which many aleadge, that they beleue
to be saued by Christe, that they haue
sufficient knowledge of their duety, and
the reste, they can supplie by their owne
diligence. Whose faithe is not so muche
(I dare saye) but they haue neede to desier with the Apostles, Lorde increase
our faithe. And if they will so confesse,
why do they forsake the chiefest means
that God hathe ordeyned, which is the
open Congregation of his people, where his worde, the fountayne of faith, is
moste purely preached, and where the
Godly examples of others maye be a
sharper spurre to prick them forward.
And as for the knowledge and diligence
of such, may be no buckler to defend
their doinges. For yf they haue those
gyftes wherof they boste, where may
they bestowe them better then in the
Churche of God? Except they will saye,
they are borne to them selues, and haue *worldly*
the gyftes of God which he would haue *respects*
comon to others, applyed to their owne *which hin*
priuate fantasie, which is to lappe them *der vs frō*
vp in a clowte, and not to put them *God oght*
forth to the vantage of the owner, as did *ded.*

p. iii.

the vnprofitable feruant: and as all
they do, to whome God hath geuen either learninge, coûfel, or worldly fubftâ
ce, which eithet for the ftréght of Cities,
pleafantneffe of ayre, trafficke or mar-
châdife, or for anie other worldely ref-
pect or politie, do abfente thê felues frô
the Congregatiô and companie of their
poore brethern, where Chrift hathe ad-
uaunced his ftandarde, and blowen his
troumpet, as is afore fayed.

Yf God then geue you not ftrength-
at the firfte to ftand in his profefsion
to the death, nor that you cannot be
quiete in confcience, abiding in your
coûtrie: you fee how his mercy hath geuen you libertie to flee, and what places he hath appoynted for you to flee
The gra- vnto, that is, were ye may do good
ces of God to your felues and others, where ye
towardes may be free from fuperftition and ido-
Englande latrie, where your faithe may be in-
are moft a creafed rather then diminifhed, and
bundant your felues ftrengthned, confirmed, and
if they wo more ftrongly armed.
uld vfe thê

But if you in taryinge will nether
ftande manfully to Chrifte your
                                    Mai-

Maifter, but betraye him with the Papiftes in doinge as they do, nor yet
with thankes vfe this remedie that God
hath graúted to oure infirmitie, to refor
te to his Churches godly iftituted: what
anfwere fhall you be able to make to
his Maieftie when he fhall call for ac-
coumpt of your doinges? How fhall
you auoyde his wrathfull indignation,
now redie to be powred vpon his enemies? Affure your felffe, they fhalbe ta
ken in there fynne: ád you alfo as God
doth fynde you. Yf in the tentes of his
enimies, doinge as they do vnder theire
ftanderde, to be ftryken with them, and
alfo to peryfhe. For in takinge part
with theire impietie, you muft be par-
takers of theire cupp likewife.

Nether is this anie newe or hard doctri
ne that may excede your capacitie,
but may rather be termed your a .b. c.
& firft principles, where in none oght
to be ignorant. That is if we wylbe
Chrifts fcholers, we moft learne to beare his croffe, & to folowe him : not
to caft it ofe our fhulders with the
enimies, and rúne from him. It is the fa-

me leſſon which of children we learned
in the Lordes prayer, that the Name of
God the Father may be ſanctified : His
kingdome come: His will be dóne. Mar
ke it brethern, that your daylie prayer
turne not to your euerlaſtinge confuſion. For yſ you daylye praye, that by
you his Name maye be ſanctified, that
is, that he may be worthely honored
for his maieſtie ád wóderfull power, reuerenced for his mercy and infinite wiſ
dome, feared for his iuſtice ád iuſte iudgemétes: and yet for feare of the vngodly, do blaſpheme his Name by diſſimu
latió ád outwarde idolatrie, are ye not
herein iudges of your owne condemnation? Prayng that his Name may be honored with your lyppes, and blaſphea-
me him in your deeds ? When you
praye that his kingdome may come,
and yet you your ſelues do buylde and
eſtabliſhe the kingdome of Satan? Whé
you deſier that his will may be donne,
and contrarie therunto, ſtudie to maintayne and accompliſhe the wil of Satan and his members?

Wherfore be nomore diſceaued
in

in so playne a matter. Yf the Lorde
be God, folow him: if Baal be God,
go after him. Playe no more the hypocrites, praye not with your lippes only,
but expresse the same in your workes.
Subiecte your selues whollye to God:
for he hath redemed you. Honor him
alone: for you are his people. Let not
the example of any leade you in to er-
rour: for men are but mortall. Truste in
the Lorde: for he is a sure rocke. Beware of his iudgementes: for they are ter-
rible. Trust not to your owne shiftes:
for they will disceaue you. Marke the
end of others, and in tyme be warned.
These lessons are harde to the fleshe,
but easie to the spirite. The waye of the
Lorde is a strayte path, but most faithefull, sure, and comfortable. In this waye
haue you also promised to walke with
Christ: and for the same cause do you
beare his Name, that you shuld forsake
the worlde and the fleshe, to yelde vnto
him all honour and obedience, before
the face of men in earthe, that he may
bestowe vpon you the glorie of his Father which is in heauen. To whom with

1.kin.19
The cōclu
sion contey
ninge the
effect of
the whole
boke.

the Sonne, and holy Ghoſt be euerlaſting prayſe, honor and glory for euemore . Amen.
From Geneua, this firſt
of Ianuarie. M.
D.LVIII.

FINIS.

WILLIAM KETHE TO
the Reader.

THe vayne harte of mã, full frayle is and blynde,
  vncerteynely setled, and rest can none fynde :
Whose hap is in wandring, to wade the wronge way,
As one apte by kinde to runne still astray.   (oght,

For, what thíge so good by truethe hathe bene wr-
Or what so well framed hath nature forth brought,
Which man is not prone by crafte to accuse,
And natures good gyftes dothe not sore abuse?

Thus see we how man, contemning Gods grace,
Is wholie inclyned, that ill shulde take place:
Whose will (truethe reiectinge) delitth that to haue,
Which nature corrupted woulde seeme still to craue.

Sith man then in iudgeinge, so thwartly is bente.
To satisfie fansie, and not true intente:
How hardly in this case, can such iudge vpright,
Whẽ trueth doth but peepe out, as semth to our sight.

Ful nedefull then were it, we had this respecte,
Before we receaue oght, or oght do reiect:
The thinge to decide so with Iudgement and skill,
That trueth may be stickler, and not our one will.

Beholde here a trueth drawne forth of her graue,
By power sore oppressed , and made a bonde slaue:
Whose chaïs, thogh this Autor could not rẽt or teare,
Yet hath he forth broght hir, in to moste clere ayer.

With whome now to reason, whoso wil assaye,
Shal learne how ill Rulers we oght to obeye.
Whiche kill, how, they care not, in their cruell rage.
Respectíg their will more, thẽ lawe, othe, or charge.

Whose fury longe fostered by suffrance and awe,
Haue right rule subuerted, and made will their lawe:
Whose pride, how to temper, this truthe will thee tell,
So as thou resiste mayste, and yet not rebell.

Rebellion is ill, to resiste is not so,
When right through resisting, is donne to that foo,
Who seeketh, but by ruine, agaynst right to raigne,
Not passinge what perishe, so she spoyle the gayne.

A publick weale wretched, and to farre disgraste,
Where the right head is of cut, and a wronge in steed
A brut beast vntamed, a misbegot then,   (plaste,
More meete to be ruled, then raigne ouer men.

A maruelous madnesse, if we well beholde,
When sighes shall assaut mē, to see them selues solde:
And yet whē frō slauery, their friēds woulde thē free,
To stick to their foes so, still slaues to be.

For France spiteth Spayne, which Englend doth
threat,
And England proud Spanyards , with salte woulde
fayne eate:
Yet Englande proud Spayne aydeth with men, ships,
and botes.
That Spayne, (France subdued once) may cut all their
throtes.

A people peruerse, repleate with disdayne,
Thogh flattrie fayne hide woulde their hate, and vile
trayne.
Whose rage, ād hotte luste, disceate, crafte, and pride,
Poore Naples their bondeslaue , with great grefe hath
tryed.

                                                    Lo,

Lo, thefe be the byrdes which Englãde mufte feede,
By plantinge of whom, to roote out their feede
Their owne landes ãd lyues, by them firfte deuourde,
Their maydes then ãd wyues, mofte vilelie deflourde.

Is this not ftronge treafon, ye vnnoble bloudds?
To ayde fuche deftroyers, both with landes ãd goods?
But when they thus pinche you, and ye put to flight,
To what forte then flee you? or where will you light?

For Englande thus folde, for Spaniardes to dwell,
Ye maye not by right, poffeffe that ye fell.
They feinge your treafon, agaynfte your owne ftate,
Wil not with theirs truft you, which they know ye
hate.

To Skotlande or France, yf ye then fhulde cry,
Your vile deeds now prefent, they may well reply,
And Dutchlãd abhorth you: this thẽ doth remayne,
Whẽ Spaniards are placed, ye mufte to newe Spayne.

But, oh dreadfull plague, ãd figne of Gods wrothe,
On fuch noble Gnatos, ftronge foes to Gods trothe.
Whom fonde feare hath framed, to prop fuch a ftaye
As countrie and people, fo feekth to betraye.

Which thinge herein proued, to be with out doute
All fuch full well finde fhall, as reade it throughout.
Yf then their hartes fayle them the right to defende,
Confufion remayneth for fuche a meete end.

Geue not thy glorie to an other: nether
that whiche is profitable for thee, to a
strange nation. Baruch. 4.

Imprinted at Geneua by Iohn Crespin,
the first of Ianuarie. Anno. D.
M. D. LVIII.